COLLECTED POEMS

Books by Veronica Forrest-Thomson

Poetry

As Veronica Forrest

Identi-kit (London: Outposts Publications, 1967)
Twelve Academic Questions (Cambridge: privately printed, 1970)

As Veronica Forrest-Thomson

Language-Games (Leeds: New Poets Award 2, School of English Press,
              University of Leeds, 1971)
Cordelia: or 'A Poem should not Mean, but Be' (Leicester: Omens
              Poetry Pamphlet no. 2, 1974)
On the Periphery (Cambridge: Street Editions, 1976)
Collected Poems and Translations (London, Lewes, Berkeley: Allardyce,
              Barnett, Publishers, 1990)
Selected Poems (Brighton: Invisible Books, 1999)

Literary Criticism

Poetic Artifice: A Theory of Twentieth-Century Poetry (Manchester:
              Manchester University Press; New York: St Martin's
              Press, 1978)

Veronica Forrest-Thomson

COLLECTED POEMS

Edited, with notes and variants, by
Anthony Barnett

Shearsman Books
in association with
Allardyce Book

This edition published in the United Kingdom in 2008 by
Shearsman Books Ltd
58 Velwell Road
Exeter EX4 4LD

in association with
Allardyce Book imprint of
Allardyce, Barnett, Publishers
14 Mount Street, Lewes
East Sussex BN7 1HL
to whom rights enquiries should be addressed

ISBN 978-1-905700-80-6

All but three of the poems in this volume were previously published in
Collected Poems and Translations (Allardyce, Barnett, Publishers, 1990). Three
of the poems were gathered in *Selected Poems* (Invisible Books, 1999).

Typeset in Aldus, with Greek in Minion.

Cover typography by AB©omposer

Contents

Editor's Note   9

Poems

Identi-kit

January Morning   13
Gemini   14
Taurus   15
Identi-kit   16
In the Greenhouse   17
Aries   18
Point of View at Noon   19
A Reaction to Rings   20
Clown (by Paul Klee)   21
In This House   22
Christmas Morning   23
Provence   24
Ambassador of Autumn (by Paul Klee)   25
The Sentence   26
Contours—Homage to Cézanne   27
According to the Script   28
Through the Looking Glass   29
Subatomic Symphony   30
Automat   32

Uncollected Early Poems

The Room   35
Sagittarius   36
Still A-Building   37
The White Magician   38
Literary Historian   41
Social Contract   42
The Needle's   43

Beginners Please   44
Epicurus   45
Don't Bite the Hand that Throws Dust in Your Eyes   47
Grapes for Grasshoppers   48
Computer 97/100 DV   49
Habitat   50
fine   51
Landscape with Yellow Birds   52
Atomic Disintegration   53
At Work: /At Play: 54
2 Staircase Poems   55
Catalog   56
Language Lesson for a Schizophrenic Age   57
Tooth   58
1,28   59
Fêtes Nationales & Zazie in the London Underground   61
The Blue Book   63
Letters of Ezra Pound   64
Epitaph for an Un-Named Priestess   65
Individuals   67
Variations from Sappho   68

Language-Games

Michaelmas   73
The Brown Book   75
Ducks & Rabbits   76
Zettel   77
Acrostic   80
Idols of the (Super)Market   81
Antiphrasis   83
Antiquities   85
Group Theory   87
The Hyphen   88
Alka-Seltzer Poem   89
Three Proper   90
Two Other   93
Criteria for Continuing a Series   94

Notes to Chapter 1,002   95
The Further-Off-From   96
Phrase Book   97
A Fortiori   98
It Doesn't Matter about Mantrippe   99

On the Periphery

In Defence of Leavis: The Common Pursuit   103
In Defence of Graham Hough: Style and Stylistics   103
The Transcendental Aesthetic   104
To R.Z. and M.W.   105
On Naming of Shadows   106
Selection Restrictions on Peanuts for Dinner   108
For the Spider who Frequents Our Bath   109
L'Effet du réel   110
An Arbitrary Leaf   111
Pfarr-Schmerz (Village-Anguish)   112
The Dying Gladiator   113
Drinks with a Mythologue   114
Address to the Reader, from Pevensey Sluice   116
On the Periphery   117
The Aquarium   118
On Reading Mr. Melville's Tales   119
Approaching the Library   120
Leaving the Library   121
Facsimile of a Waste Land   122
Pastoral   123
Not Pastoral Enough   124
Le Signe (Cygne)   125
Conversation on a Benin Head   126
The Ear of Dionysios: Ode   127
Le Pont traversé: Ode   130
In Memoriam Ezra Pound   132
Strike   134
The Lady of Shalott: Ode   136
The Garden of Proserpine   138
Sonnet   141

Further Poems

A Plea for Excuses   145
Since the Siege and Assault Was Ceased in Troy . . .   146
I have a little hour-glass   148
I have a little nut-tree   148
In Memoriam   149
Canzon   150
Cordelia: or, 'A Poem Should not Mean, but Be'   152
Richard II   158
S/Z   160
Lemon and Rosemary   162

Appendices

1: An Impersonal Statement   164
2: Contributor's Note   165
3: Note to *Language-Games*   165
4: Preface to *On the Periphery*   166
5: Richard II   168

Bibliography & Recordings

A: Dissertation & Published Literary Criticism   170
B: Published Letters   171
C: Personal Tributes to the Author   171
D: Sound Recordings   172

Notes   173

Index of Titles   185

EDITOR'S NOTE

This volume reprints all the poems, except translations, by Veronica Forrest-Thomson in her *Collected Poems and Translations* (1990) with the addition of three early poems discovered since then, which were included as an appendix to her *Selected Poems* (1999).

Here, as in the 1990 edition, *Collected* means all poems published previously as books together with all those uncollected poems published in periodicals or similar, or deposited in a public archive, that have been traced. Also included are a number of apparently unpublished poems taken from the manuscripts and typescripts that remain among her personal papers. Not included are early poems, apparently unpublished in her lifetime, written before the poems gathered in her first volume *Identi-kit* (1967): a selection of such poems will be found under the title 'Poems of Youth' in *Adam International Review*, vol. xxxix, nos. 391–393 (London, 1975). Nor have later apparently unfinished drafts or fragments of poems been included.

Before the publication of *Language-Games* (1971) the author published her poems under the name Veronica Forrest. An exception is the poem 'Reaction to Rings' published under her full name (which she chose to hyphenate, contrary to family practice) in the *Glasgow Herald*, 10 September 1966.

Veronica Forrest-Thomson was both a poet and a critical theorist. A bibliography of her literary criticism is included here. There exists among her personal papers a typescript dated '*c*.1963', with manuscript additions dated 1966, in which she sets out her ideas, projects and purposes for poetry. She wrote several commentaries to accompany the publication or public reading of her poetry; the 'Note' to *Language-Games* and the 'Preface' to the posthumously published *On the Periphery* have been removed from their original positions in those volumes and brought together with related pieces in the appendices.

Obvious errors in transcription or in printing have been corrected silently in those poems that have been published previously. *Selected Poems* corrected a number of typos in *Collected Poems and Translations*. Most were not mischievous but *Identi-Kit* for *Identi-kit* was. In preparing this new *Collected* further typos were found, including a couple carried over from the author—'Agammemnon', surely. It cannot be said with certainty that others have not been overlooked or accidentally introduced. Notification of such will be gratefully received.

The author's idiosyncratic use of the hyphen, greatly important to her, has been respected. Accurate formatting of some poems has not always been easy to determine or to adhere to. Where there are doubts about the author's intentions, her typescripts, where available, have usually been the guide; otherwise, if clarification seemed necessary, details will be found in the 'Notes' to this volume. Some published variants are also described, and sources given for them as well as for previously uncollected poems. For other poems, periodical publication generally has not been noted.

This volume attempts to gather all the author's mature poetry but it is possible that a few other poems are still to be discovered. For example, only two issues of the Liverpool University poetry magazine *Equator*, some or all the issues of which were edited by the author, have been traced. Some extant letters with typescripts or manuscripts have proved inaccessible, so it cannot be ascertained whether unknown poems or variants are to be found there. This edition differs from the earlier *Collected* in respect of ordering. There, the decision was taken to position early poems at the end of the book. Here, the ordering is, more or less, chronological.

Collected Poems and Translations and *Selected Poems* contain acknowledgements to all those who generously assisted with the preparation of those volumes. My renewed thanks to them and my apologies that, but for one, their names are not repeated here.

I would like to thank Jonathan Culler, executor of the author's literary estate, for his graciousness in allowing me to prepare this new edition of Veronica Forrest-Thomson's poetry.

Anthony Barnett
Lewes, April 2008

Identi-kit

(1967)

to Liz Cullington

JANUARY MORNING

Hot ha'penny sun pressed copper
against the frozen-window sky;
a metallic sunbeam falls
with a clank of light across the eye.

The world is winched on an iron chain,
then whirled on a wheel of frost.

Gables' only purpose to maintain
angle of a shadow flat and clear
slanting the bright sharp snow.
Birdsong rattles over the slates,
a sudden jangling skeleton of sound;
is still.

The world is clamped in a frigid crate
and notched silent, on a stone.

Brittle air crackles beneath the breath.
Corners, as black triangles, converge
perspectiveless to point the air,
congealing clinging along the surfaces,
bleaching house contours against the sky.
All that moves is a jet-trail slicing
silver across the red-cold sky.

The world is pierced by a steel-white spear,
and nailed to a cross of ice.

GEMINI

When all's said and spun,
heads or tails?
it's all two
for I am a pun
on someone unknown.

My life's his uncracked code.
Pleasure consists only in deflecting
the signals he transmits,
trying to flex his wit reflected
through my reflexes.

Thus we play a game
in which each day is a lost bet,
for how, when I must use his words,
can I communicate my paradox
to a distinctive third.

I'll never break true the mirror
that lies in each it and you,
in which I can see just me,
watching him,
watching me.

TAURUS

I have copper's valency
and can transform most elements
to alloys of stability,
if Venus puts me on my metal;
but mostly I reserve my nature,
wearing attributes like ornaments
—pretty things appeal—
but happiest chewing time.
Browsing in the fine collection
of my past surely I should find
the future built around me
like a home.

IDENTI-KIT

Love is the oldest camera.
Snap me with your eyes.
Wearied with myself I want
a picture that simplifies.

Likeness is not important
provided the traits cohere.
Dissolve doubts and contradictions
to leave the exposure clear.

Erase shadows and negative
that confuse the tired sight.
Develop as conclusive definition
a pattern of black and white.

For I wish to see me reassembled
in that dark-room of your mind.

IN THE GREENHOUSE

Entering the dim air where edges
are furred like geranium leaves,
the mind blurs in sympathy,
the line dividing plant and primate,
until to think seems out of place.

By a definition suited
to the dissecting room of intellect,
furled fiddleheads of fern
are gametophytes in pteropsida,
but here reduced suddenly
to a creature in the primeval wood,
I remember only that they are edible.

Orchids, commended in science
as illustrating the complexity of evolution,
seem now to elude even their simple name.
Each self-contained, the patterns
of naming and of being run parallel
like two planes that can never touch.

The silent rhythm of pulsating pores
filling my lungs with filtered earth
is all I feel or know of alien shapes
that once were flowers.
I breathe their breath
until all definitions are dissolved,
and homo sapiens is nothing more to me.

ARIES

Slid like a bead along the bowstring
of its orbit, earth tilts the sun
till, at the first point of a red planet,
it strikes on the equator like a match
to light the year; ignites

a will stalled in civilised complexity,
slips the mind-machine into first gear
and sends it, refuelled with simple self,
back to hunt in dreams a life
whose heart secret can be pierced
conquered and bleeding by a spear.

Batteries recharged by the perennial illusion
that sap rises in a life as in a flower,
rupture themselves with revs of energy
trying to electrify the unconducive days.
Hysterical tremors of spring insinuate
that purposes are knives
to sharpen on events, clear-cutting
as the incision of the equinox.

POINT OF VIEW AT NOON

Stilled by weight of sunshine
fixing their contours in a mould
of light, lime trees
have gestures as convulsively immobile
as a Byzantine ikon;
and mosaics of mottled leaves
are pressed into the air, set,
not to be shattered by wind
that has to do with time.

Framed in an unblinking eye
the scene seems no more living
or capable of movement
than the turquoise tendrils traced
on this quiet vase
which holds severed roses
red against the blue enamelled sky.

A REACTION TO RINGS

A pale-green thought in a jade ellipse
at the finger tips;
the motto of all rings, "it will pass."
Alas, the gentle susurration of the past.
The mind sets love ill a diamond "forever"
which will mock moreover the death of love.

A pearl-pale thought with the opal tone,
half-coloured of what has gone
and has been half-forgotten.
Milk tear and silver angles grip
the only fact, their own reality;
an irony,
that this metal circle's called eternity.

A rustless static dark-green thought
blood-shot
contrasts the flow of blood beneath which rots;
is harder than skeleton against this fragile flesh.
The crowns of decomposing hands
whose lives' constituents are dust,
all except gold and stone
alone.

CLOWN (BY PAUL KLEE)

Seen in the wink, a link (with)
green flaunt, too clear in face (of)
shadows which do not appear;
a jaunty impulse, yet boxed,
looped (also) in

a curve idling, a sidle into
an angle, stencilled by heat;
       hot thought read through
       red through red thought
       what not?

a whatnot leer
clear in nose swerve, in
blue insinuate grin let in
seen within (is) a view
somewhat askew;
          and you?

IN THIS HOUSE

All the photographs are faded.
All the clocks are slow.
Last year's words lie stale like smoke
on used up air; the piano keys
are touched only to be dusted.
Rooms and furnishings
have been so long familiar
that they are merely memories;
and now is happening elsewhere.

But, habit being a substitute for will,
though the mirrors are tired of our faces,
and spring comes later each year,
we go on lighting flowers like candles
at windows dissolved by rain.

CHRISTMAS MORNING

A gull curved like a boomerang
slants the sky, tilting
the horizon with surge of snow
muffling eye and ear.
Its thin scream rattles the rigid twigs.
Trees stand shrunk
under the crouching clouds, worshipping
nothing.

And our packed houses
spires and lights so proudly
planted seem no more
than a huddle of grey tents
on the edge of the waiting mist.

PROVENCE

Aeons of sun, ages of men
make tree-trunks of stone
and bark-coloured bricks,
earth weary of feet,
life weary and gay.

Mosaics of flesh
and kaleidoscope streets
seem brilliant in perpetual noon
till dark drains warm bronze
grey as the faces
on sarcophagi.

Strong swords of cypress
point a landscape at prime,
but pillars now shuttered
once framed the same sky
and fertile land is manured
by decay.

Light dissolves future
like outlines of forms
and shifts focus to
a camp of survivors who linger
sipping the south
in a graveyard café.

AMBASSADOR OF AUTUMN (BY PAUL KLEE)

Year's spectrum modulates
around the centre spectre.
Each single moment's tone
appears alone, yet signals
the gradation in the air
towards the centre spectre;

clears a half-uncovered curve
cold moon, negative reflector
of the centre spectre,

where gold reflects last light
frost-focused against white,
frail parody of sun.
Leaf held to itself firm
in pattern's final thread
about to snap,
fulfilled as things only may
whose sole future is decay.

THE SENTENCE

You taught me language, left me with words in hand
to spin their critical cocoon around a life
which others lead, which I can merely understand,
caught in a web of maybe, ought, and if;

for, disengaged in the act of articulation
from the initiating spontaneity,
it disdains the direct communication
of a kiss or coition or a warning cry;

exist to exorcise by implication
the amorphous impulses of beast and bird
which, when in need of explication,
must manage without benefit of word.

Its narcissistic joy defines a world deformed by form
where diagnosis is the sickness, the patient, the nurse
to whom sterilisation is perception's norm;
but now, at least, I know how to curse.

CONTOURS—HOMAGE TO CÉZANNE

Pattern, like a magnetic field,
is passionate in restraint; limits compress
significance; framed energy is sealed.
Objects, having nothing to express

except themselves, attain intensity
in assumed balance, which alleges,
in face of our amorphous liberty,
the joy of everything with edges.

But these tight contours owe
shape and definition to the eye
of inessential man who

from complication learns to simplify,
fuse form with what alone forms cannot show,
and in this act becomes as sure as they.

ACCORDING TO THE SCRIPT

Encounter with a friend, acquaintance
or just someone in a bar
is merely a pretext to display
your theory of what you are.

Absorbed in your own performance
you applaud or criticise,
and only to watch your reflection
do you look into his eyes.

Or, if a contrast's noticed,
it's to serve as a backcloth
useful for the setting
and to show your costume off.

He thought you concentrating
when you were running through
your lines rehearsing gestures
while waiting for your cue.

Still soliloquising you said goodbye,
went on, and never knew
that the stranger, the other
had been speaking to you.

THROUGH THE LOOKING GLASS

Mirror, mirror on the wall
show me in succession all
my faces, that I may view
and choose which I would like as true.

Teach me skill to disguise
what's not pleasing to the eyes,
with faith, that life obeys the rules,
in man or God or football pools.

Always keep me well content
to decorate attitude and event
so that somehow behind the scene
I may believe my actions mean;

that one can exercise control
in playing out a chosen role;
rub clouded glass and then,
at will, write self on it again.

But if, in some unlucky glance,
I should glimpse naked circumstance
in all its nowhere-going-to,
may you crack before I do.

SUBATOMIC SYMPHONY

I

Subatomic particles
revolve in supersonic whirls,
inaudible to the eye
for their frequency's too high,
invisible to the ear
as light can make them disappear.

Resting in their mass
protons throb heavy as a double bass.
Nuclear notes resonate
in echo-chambers of atomic space,
their tone dependent on
meson disintegration.

The planetary suite
of electrons keeps the beat
with saxophonic wails
in wave-cycles of piano scales,
uncertain of the time
to punctuate a flowing line.

Out of tune
like a touch on a drum
a falter of pulse
vibrates through the long taut chord
of the bass.

Rhythm sways
to the throb of decay;
nucleons jar,
unbound from the force
of their backing bars;

rebound and release
the discord of magnetic clash.
Showers of neutron percussion smash
through the twang
of a too-tight string.

Swung to sound by their spin
overtone neutrinos whine.
The saxophone picks up the theme
as jets of electrons in a high-speed scream.

III

Plucked by a lower pitch
strings' vibrations
modulate down.
Sounds pitched at a lower key
regain stability.

Their pulse like a metronome
pulls the electrons in.
Each orbit jump carried on
a piano wave quantum.

With atomic number
as key signature, tune resolves
material notes of mass
and energy underneath
spreading like ripples of breath.

AUTOMAT

To problems of communication
there's a rational approach
in the world of conversation
analysing dialogue and role.

In this circumstantial jigsaw
we're pieces that can fit,
being each properly equipped
with a well-stocked relationship kit.

Whose main tool's insight that explains
how and why each incident arose.
Meaning motive attitude, even obsolescence
are built in every pre-packaged pose.

Unprecedented patterns alter image and technique
but it's comforting to know,
when perplexed by presentation that
experience's a practised P.R.O.

Thus the individual ego (once called a soul)
must learn to let the transcendental go;
find fulfilment pulling puppet strings
and putting on an entertaining show.

Uncollected Early Poems

THE ROOM

The air, so whitened   by the sun
that it's hard to tell where the light ends
and glass begins, is veined   by smoke
like   marble; life is a cigarette
puffed   by time; history an ashtray.

Once some surge of thought or feeling
welded these miscellaneous furnishings
into a mirror of the mind's   moment
reflected in their polished significance.

But now the timelessness of the inanimate
negates it;   the past, irrelevant
as death is to funeral ornaments,
has held nothing of them;
and the corpse coffined in an armchair
of memories is imperfectly embalmed by thought;
For objects slide   so quickly through the years
that already I'm beginning to decay.

SAGITTARIUS

Something dislocates.
I find me trying, to be
without a predicate.
For once a blueprint is no guarantee
against anonymity.

The self-set questionnaire
of circumstance
can't make all square.
Aspects jar.
A day with jagged edges and
minutes sharp to breathe through
bars retreat to neat
articulation;

derides the jingling skeletons
of sounds I blame
for these complexities:
Mercury, Moon, Jupiter,
when I was born,
were placed all wrong.
Sometimes the stars' perplexities
are fun, but now, not even names,
just pain; thoughts hurt.

The mind's an aggravated boil,
needs lancing; but no tool
—unless maybe
these jigsaw shards
of useless personality.

At last I can forget
the self-made self and work
to turn the spheres and all
that matters of "I am"
into this it
that is.

STILL A-BUILDING

Succinct as algebra
Concrete cubes and squares
Itself to root in space.

Structures, their forces raised
To the power of zero, dissect
Themselves with glass.

Cranes translate equations
Into joint of hoist and strut; recalculate
The slide's rule in multiples

Of stone sections
A re-solution seeming to vindicate
Trust in a system

That can fit symbol to steel
Make mathematics mediate
Between concept and cement

And express unknown in known
As stresses that reciprocate,
Value of forces in two dimensions
—equilibrium.

THE WHITE MAGICIAN

I

Oh Leonardo
do
you
know how
to screw
do you
no

how
the kite's tail
brushed
your mouth
at birth
and flew
to Milan
and back
again

playing Condottieri
tell us why
anything ever was begun
while learning how
to die
mechanics of anatomy
why try
to understand
a left hand.

If self is functionality,
Batman can do
better than you
so Leonardo
screw you
too.

II

A batwing's swing
stretches your brainspan,
spaceman,

draws our sinews'
twisting threads
to a spinning head.

Revolving blades
wind in the tensions
of light and shade.

Birds that soar
on your drawing board
never left ground,

for the work is done
when eye and object
became one.

But we can't tell you if any thing . . .
in our blueprint world,
a beholder's eye

blinds with the cataracts
behind that desperate flatness
of her smile.

III

Oh Leonardo
do
you
show how
to know
do you
no

how
Ludovico Sforza
thought so
of the lady
whose throat
you slit open with a stoat,
or Cesare Borgia
made war.
They were
too muddled for you.

Whose helicopter
dropped her
in the cup at the last supper,
the virgin on the rocks
of thought.

There are vineyards in Tuscany;
but oh Leonardo,
how can we about to die,
show you
why.

LITERARY HISTORIAN

I remember them saying,
these poems, their something
for someone at sometime
for me too, at one time.

That got in the way;
so I sent them away
back into history—
just temporarily.

They won't come back now.
I can't remember how
the words spoke, or what
they said,
except:
We are all dead.

SOCIAL CONTRACT

I'll blow smoke in your eyes
if you'll blow smoke in mine.
Light up; relax;
cigarette packs
enclose guarantees
of social ease.
Strike the right note
with a match
and fill the gaps
in communication
by inhalation
of instant pseudo-sympathy.
A brand-name's a shorthand
for identity.
Squirt out, like a squid,
your smokescreen of pride
to hide
hopes and needs we can't express
and turn out the inside.
We'll fill the ashtrays
of the day's
conviviality, and part,
stubbing out our fag ends
in each other's heart.

THE NEEDLE'S

threaded 'I' seams (and seems) me
into shape; stitches styles
to fit its dressmaker's dummy
which, without a full-stocked wardrobe
would fall, formless
back into the un-darned whole
of inarticulate experience;

round which we pin
our paper-patterns of identity
designed to make self wearable
and placeable within
the patchwork of personality
where we cut hem fray tear
or just adjust each other's clothes.

For you do not sharpen
to the steel-plated point
that pierces intermittently metallic
through circumstantial gathers and embroideries;
and must protectively prepare
to look distinguished in meetings with reality,
or leave your face as well
behind you, folded on the chair.

BEGINNERS PLEASE

In flats libraries and pubs
—so many greenrooms where
greasepaint taints the atmosphere
with scents of self-absorption—
they wait for the curtain call.
Even lovers communicate in stage whispers,
gestures aimed at the audience of extras
behind the footlights in a coffee bar.
Needing a producer
for a whole personality,
without anyone to ask if it's a farce
or tragedy,
each rehearses for an unknown part
in a play still to be written.

The future, an agent, will arrange for them
a crowd scene to be secure in,
a star to understudy,
a musty retreat among discarded props,
or the fascination of a lifetime
in the wardrobe trying on role after role;
will teach each to forget the hope to find
a costume individually designed,
a make-up mask to perfect but not distort
the face behind,
a script of acts to match
complexities of mind;
and of stepping from the wings
without self-doubt or stage-fright,
clarified and held by a full moment's spotlight,
into a performance of complete articulate
reality,
in which thoughts fit in patterns like ballet,
no move is mistimed,
and all the banal lines come out
quite different.

EPICURUS

Dare I eat some cheese,
since it's Panathenaia,
toffee-tasting goat cheese
stinking like old Diogenes;
might cause dyspepsia or even appendicitis.
Dare I risk some wine;
a half-glass hung me over
last time.
Pleasure is such an exacting discipline.
Whatsisname
who said something about
"burning with a hard gemlike flame"
knew the score
in the trials of an empirical connoisseur.

But nowadays
the idea seems to raise
response without responsibility.
They don't show
much taste, Alcibiades and co.
Hippies miniskirts drug parties,
sunstruck by the dazzle of bright surfaces,
sensation without sense.
It's true,
reality is mind-reflecting surfaces all through
(a rare treat, this honey from Hymettos)
but to play kottabos
with one's life thus . . .

To stay dégagé
and yet to play,
that I could dream of.
Give one's eyes to nature
for a mirror.
Reflection of a raindrop in the moon,
an actor making rules and game

subject and object the same,
aesthesis path at prolepsis,
focused by the security of doubt
tuned lyre-like
for the key to each sensation.
Tune in, turn on, drop out
(as I believe they would phrase it)

Have I changed desire, anxiety's death
for fear of life,
its shifting-toned complexity
in which a self is found or lost.
The game is hide and seek.
What do you think Hermarchos?
too dangerous,
a blind man's buff?
No, Hermarchos please,
just a little bit of bread and no cheese.

DON'T BITE THE HAND THAT THROWS DUST IN YOUR EYES

Tit for tat
spits the cat-black
kettle at
a watched pot that
never boils.

Bird in hand's worth
dog and bitch
in manger which
will never save our stitch
in time.

The wise child knows
an ill wind blows
storms up
in his dad's teacup
but no half-breadfruit
falls far from its tree.

Between frying pan and deep blue sea
let you and me
make hay
while in sunless places
the human race is
cutting off its noses to spite its faces.

GRAPES FOR GRASSHOPPERS

Why do you walk through the world in gloves
Oh fat white lady whom nobody loves?

I'm looking for gift horses in the grass,
hack press or piebald ideas with pass-
words to let me in to this pretty kettle of vipers.

All you'll get is a snake in the neck.
Take thorns from flesh and cricks from tongue;
pick your hand out of the plough while you're young.

I can't throw stones from castles in air
or send smoke signals without a fire.
I must join in writing on this side of the wall.

There's no making omelettes without breaking glass;
stir with a square peg that gathers no moss;
suck each day like an egg—Teach that to your gran—
then simmer it all in your own frying pan.
Polish a long spoon to taste your own truth;
for too many cooks are spoiling the broth.

COMPUTER 97/100 DV

I salute your translation of
"The spirit is willing but the flesh is weak"

The ghost is ready but the meat is raw

our ghost
            in the machine
makes neuron patterns on a television screen

The cost is steady but the heat is saw

McLuhan's touch
completes the form for "Operation Match"

The lost is really but the meet is law

Cross-circuiting
re-structures the limbo of a "thing"

The most is usually but treat is know

Binary systems go.
For our inside is out to show

in that sex orgy
            technology

HABITAT

a bus
shelters

broken window
pains

telephones
shadow-box
(trying to connect us)

stone flags
waver
trip feet
in heat

the street
gutters out
in building sights

—These are
our outside
of enough

fine
finite
finesse
in fine, finitess
infinitess
infiniteness
infinitesimal
finesse in
infinite mess

LANDSCAPE WITH YELLOW BIRDS

```
      v                             s
     is                            bk
    k feel                     bird   f ly
   yellow                      s       u
     e l                       kopey  e
     e l                       eye
   sk op
     we


                ?                        by
                                          i
                                         s r
   birds                                weed
   leafly                               s   a
   a    i                               h s r
   d    c                               shaped
   e   ye                               by  dy
   s   es                               e   oe
       l                                s   wl
       l                                    l
      no                                   no
      ww                                    w
```

ATOMIC DISINTEGRATION
3 variations on the "Smashed Atom" theme

(1–visual)

(2–vocal)

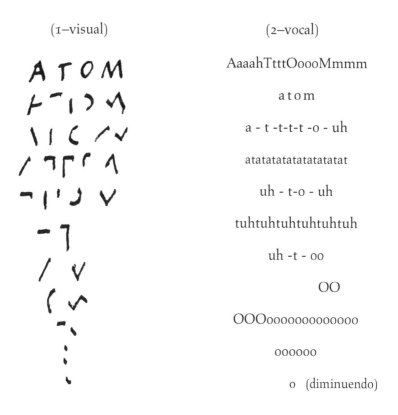

AaaahTtttOoooMmmm

a t o m

a - t -t-t-t -o - uh

atatatatatatatatatat

uh - t-o - uh

tuhtuhtuhtuhtuhtuh

uh -t - oo

OO

OOOooooooooooooooo

oooooo

o   (diminuendo)

(3—for mass performance) any number of people (1) repeat in unison several times clearly the word ATOM (2) repeat ATOM at different times out of unison (like a part song) (3) out of synchronisation repeat in staccato way the individual letters A-T-O-M ending in an unintelligible babble.

At Work: Na

W?   W?   W?

Re   At   Tc   I   Mn   Br   F   Cl   H

H

W?   W?   W?

Cr   Se   Mo   Te   Po   S   O

O

$2Na + 2H_2O$

$2NaOh + H_2$

Ah!

At Play: He   He   He

Pb   Pd   Pt

Bi   2i   Xe   Se

ScCsScCsScCs

Ht   Hg   Ht   Hg

Kr

Cocu

Cocu

Cocu

Psclak!

2 STAIRCASE POEMS

l
l
hel
ixestriangl
les
lipstespira
l
l
l
l
l

sil

ver

esc

ala

tor

sta

ple

s
cal

es

ilv
ers
tap
les
cal
ato
r

CATALOG

THE TEACHINGS OF THE COMPASSIONATE BUDDHA
library of congress catalog card number
THE WISDOM OF THE HOLY TALMUD
library of congress catalog card number
THE ETHICS OF ARISTOTLE
library of congress catalog card number
THE DIVINE COMEDY OF DANTE
library of congress catalog card number
THE RELATIVITY OF EINSTEIN
library of congress catalog card number
THE WESTERN DECLINE OF SPENGLER
library of congress catalog card number
THE CAPITAL OF KARL MARX
library of congress catalog card number

53-91745   2-6334   70-6199
6-9932   39-0019

SHUFFLE WELL BEFORE COMMENCING PLAY

LANGUAGE LESSON FOR A SCHIZOPHRENIC AGE

The pen is on the table.
The pen is not on the table.
The writing is on the wall.
The writing is not on the wall.
The table is on the floor.
The table is not on the floor.
The heart is in the mouth.
The heart is not in the mouth.
The bull is in the china-shop.
The bull is not in the china-shop.
The tongue is in the cheek.
The tongue is not in the cheek.
The room is in the sky.
The car is in the sea.
The man is in the moon.
The man is on the woman.
The man is on the man.
The woman is on the man.
The woman is on the woman.
not not not not not
God is in his heaven.

TOOTH

I'm an old mouth at this game.
Summer without an apisectomy just wouldn't seem the same.
The tensions of the world compressed between the chair
and that little grey square
of windowed air.
Battles, defeats, victories
open wider please.
On the intimate excitement of mini-crises:
an abscess that turned out to be three,
one post and crown
that crumbled down.
Another bit through;
as the filling seeps out of a self.
We're told contemporary ills
are due to deprivation of atavistic thrills.
But as a testing ground I'd swop
war, love, crime, politics or every tenuous perfected skill
for that yearly duel with the drill.
Because each time I give my name
to the receptionist,
who knows if I'll get back the same
when post-impressionist?
There's more than jaws remodelled or recast.
Identity is lost
and fought for during each half-hour.
And how can I be sure
of reconstructing the framework of that smile
I left behind me at the door.

1, 28

Sprinkle a pinch of dust, or three,
on Archytas F.R.S.
who specialised in nebulae;
memorial—an out-of-date laboratory.
Tantalus studies divinity
transubstantiating our family flesh;
prefers the gods out of reach.
Lord Chief Justice Minos
was not given leave to appeal.
Pythagoras believed in reincarnation
hence lost only bones nerves blood brain.
The rest of him's still waiting.

As you pass their floating corpses, astronaut,
erase especially unnecessary words;
"But wholly one the night remains,
death's road to be walked once for all".
How unremarkable that
"Furies serve some as a spectacle for Mars"
or "The greedy sea is a destruction to sailors",
phrases whose only use is in a grammar.
Predicatively dative
we define function not being.
Death is not immortalised by apostrophe
or life by ideas.
We know our place, Horatius,
better even than you;
find nothing incongruous in
"Minds about to die
measuring the innumerable sands of stars",
claim no immunity
from dust storms meteorites magnetic shift,
because we have them all worked out.
Facts do not need emotion.

Thus: please don't clutter up the sky
with littered personality.
I know you're in a hurry, but anyway
you don't have long;
so pulverise the past dear
before you hurry on.

FÊTES NATIONALES & ZAZIE IN THE LONDON UNDERGROUND

"July: I would have painted
in a yellow jacket eating cherries."
je m'en fiche de toutes ces affiches, icons
of worship on Boul' Mich. As the incense
of Gauloises burns these saints
of the new dispensation are haloed
in self-approbation although
THE PRESENT KING OF FRANCE IS BALD
Sur le plan du Métro it is clear
just where we want to go,
that one may claim reassurance
from a multicoloured name, objective
design from an abstract line although
one may écrire n'importe où
sont les noms de yester-year?
(les noms d'antan sont n'importe où)
Bien que on songe
à cette mélange des langues and hear
a quotation for every occasion, cliché
or paradox, with a coin in the intellectual jukebox
(if one can find a bureau de change)
si l'on a de la chance de trouver
la station de correspondance
for the verbal dance, de raccrocher
"In a station of the Metro"
ce passant, the apparition
of the literary tradition, still
THE PRESENT KING OF FRANCE IS BALD
et le quatorze juillet
on paie what is due to our nostalgie
de la boue avec les mots
qui coûtent trop. Phrases
come too dear for where
are the words of yester-year?
The rate of exchange between thing
and sign devalues a currency

of mental outline so then there is love
dancing wine et tous les restes
du second-best, et, as one can,
l'on se sauve parce que
LE ROI PRESENT DE LA FRANCE EST CHAUVE

*(Opening quotation from Dr. Johnson's Dictionary;
refrain from philosophical discussions on "referring",
on the connection between thing and sign.)*

THE BLUE BOOK

Thus party with witte
party with nygraumancy
King's College is on fire;
I have an image of dining in Hall with Dr. Dee.
We shall talk at a later occasion
of the way in which words and things may be connected.
Tonight we should like to say,
What the picture tells us is itself,
This language-game is played
instead of, We have this experience.

It patterns facts, names, architecture, dates
(As in the lawcourts in Paris
a motor accident is represented
by means of dolls.)
A context in which we occur
—"the slightly hysterical style of University talk"—
teaches us our meaning;
a fourth dimension for the blue
of that bound typescript.

The gap between red and green
is then grammatical;
white objects through coloured spectacles.
But though our syntax stains the window-glass,
those stones across the court
assert their tenses
party per fess argent and vert,
party per chevron or and gueules.

In order to be clear about aesthetic words
you have to describe ways of living.
said Wittgenstein
                    who was "indifferent to his surroundings".
remembering the date (1969) on the calendar
an attempt to condense the James novel
(a young American T.S. Eliot,
write him at Merton, Oxford.
I think him worth watching
                    and
his *Portrait of a Lady* is very nicely drawn.)
in the literary scene of Allen Ginsberg
(Apocalyptic tradition of Whitman, of course)
could only be tried here
(If you people at Cam can do
                    anything
in the way of a milieu.)
The need of old forms, old situations,
as Yeats wrote (1929)
                    also,
Ezra when he recreates Propertius
escapes from his scepticism.
Whether "historical or philosophical" in approach
this is still
some form of exercise that don't depend
on the state of your liver;
the bus late an idea in labour
and no pencil or paper
(but to dial 999 for an ambulance that night
was much more exciting.)

I don't believe in personal relationships,
said the young anthropologist
                    (female),
I believe in fantasy.
But to fall in love with one's teachers
that also is a matter of economy.

EPITAPH FOR AN UN-NAMED PRIESTESS

There are not enough nouns around which to create images.
For verbs express activity and the act
is unambiguous. Experience is an active
verb. Mummy and Coffin of an Un-named
Priestess (*c.*1050 B.C.). There are not
enough pronouns to create images around.
Only the ivory handle of a bronze mirror,
said the Lady
of Shalott.
Now we move on to the Cycladic Antiquities.
Marble figure of a woman from Cambridge
(*c.*1969 A.D.). "Such a comparison *might*
help to show that common fundamental
sculptural ideas persist." (Antiparos 2500–
2000 B.C.) (Henry Moore 1969 A.D.).
The simplicity of wedge on ovoid, nose
in face and the functionality of buttocks
is belied by a shifting poise and glitter
an instability of marble. I am, however, sick
of mirrors. And metaphor is a *low* relief.
Manuscript Room, Bassae Room, Tea &
Coffee Room.
                    But all I mean
                    is that no-one
                    wants to be deceived
                    in his own mind.
(Plato, *Republic* II *c.*380 B.C.). Monochrome
is a desired medium though they coloured
their statues and we colour our
dreams
                    In things which touch
                    most nearly the most
                    important part of him
                    no man really wants
                    to be deceived but
                    is terrified of it.

But there *aren't* enough names. So what
is left except fiction, verbal activity
being too crude for us. The act
is ambiguous (vide supra). To leave
a clay jar inscribed "Megakles
is handsome" and signed by "Phistias
as potter" since
>we have already
>forbidden madness
>and the representation
>of madness,
is the alternative to mummification. It
is the poised instability of marble. So,
of the second case "in which the poet speaks
in his own person", "the best example
is lyric poetry". Although "A man cannot
play many characters as well as he can, one",
this statue of an un-named *person* (There are
not enough pronouns.) is carved in imitation
of Cycladic Art and in compassion
for Egyptian Metonymies.

INDIVIDUALS

are complex
            not as a tangle of wire
but as a coiled spring
            before it is stretched out
into simplicity.
            Strawson's cat slices
slip through your fingers
            with a prickle of fur;
basic particulars:
            persons
and material bodies.
            Pound's cats at Rapallo
too hungry to bother
            with their place in a conceptual scheme
appear nevertheless
            in the Cantos
"some of them are so ungrateful"
said T.S. Eliot.

            Practical Cats
can omit
            "the exasperating clause":
"if all objectivity and all knowledge is relative . . . "
            Mr. Eliot
never returned to take his doctor's degree.
("Forty six years after my academic philosophizing
   came to an end, I find myself unable to think
   in the terminology of this essay. Indeed
   I do not claim to understand it.")
He
   slips through your fingers
            with a prickle of fur.
   But there is at least a case
            that poetry should trace
   the double helix
   (those interlocking strands of DNA)
            before it try
   to straighten the spring.

VARIATIONS FROM SAPPHO

1

mingled with all manner of colours
mingled withall manner of colours
minglad with allmanner of colours
mengladwith all mingled of colours
man glad withall mangled of colours
manglad with all mingle of call ours

2

```
          heart                    altogether
I can                                      shine back
                    shall be to me
                    shall be to me
          heart                    altogether
I can                                      shine back
```

3

```
        It is not you who are to me
        it is          who are to me
            is not
                you who are
                            to me
        it is not                 me
                    who?
```

4

You burn me
Yu   born my
  o   u   y
You bore me
  w   h   y

5

a(ll) mi(xed)
te(ll) tongue (me)
tell to(ngue) ( )
t(all)
les(s)

Language-Games

(1971)

MICHAELMAS

daisy:
        garden aster of a shrubby habit
October:
                bearing masses of small purplish flowers
blackbird:
                the ring ouzel
crocus:
            the autumn crocus
moon:
        the
        harvest
        moon

Michaelse maesse her on lande wunode
se eorl syththan oth thet ofer sce
in 1123
        masses of small purplish flowers
        the ring ouzel
        the autumn crocus
        the
        harvest
        moon

tide:
      time
spring:
        Indian Summer
term:
        a term or session of the High Court of Justice
        in England and also of Oxford,
        Cambridge

the kinges power and is ost wende vorth
to Oxenforde aboute mielmasse

in 1297
     time
     Indian summer
     also of Oxford, Cambridge
     at the gret cowrtes at Mykelmas the year
     in 1453
          Trinity
          Nevile's
          Queens'
              and
bearing masses of small purplish flowers
the harvest
moon.

(All quotations from the OED.*)*

THE BROWN BOOK

But in a fairy tale the pot too can hear and see[1]
and help the hero on his way[2]
to stimulate something to thoughts of his own,
Noms de Personnes, Noms de Pays

as Proust taught le tout Paris
his little phrase
trying to get between pain and its expression.[3]
Life lies between Combray and Illiers.[4]

It is not impossible reflections in a madeleine
bring light into one brain[5, 6]
but a man who wants discrete particulars[7]
cries out in pain

with the asphasiac surface of a day's
objects and events,
can only choose the mouth which says:[8]
I should have liked to produce a good book.

This has not come about
but the time is past in which I could improve it.

[1] Certainly but it can also talk
[2] But of course it is not likely
[3] We are not concerned with the difference, internal/external
[4] Language-game no. 30
[5] Or another
[6] In its poverty and in the darkness of lost time
[7] When the light strikes Fizeau's mirror
[8] A stamp which marks them mine.

(Quotations freely adapted from
Brown Book, Investigations, *and Proust.)*

DUCKS & RABBITS

in the stream;[1]
look, the duck-rabbits swim between.
The Mill Race
at Granta Place
tosses them from form to form,
dissolving bodies in the spume.

Given A and see[2]
find be[3]
(look at you, don't look at me)[4]
Given B, see A and C.
that's what metaphor[5]
is for.

Date and place
in the expression of a face[6]
provide the frame
for an instinct to rename,[7]
to try to hold apart
Gestalt and Art.

[1] Of consciousness
[2] The expression of a change of aspect is the expression of a new perception.
[3] And at the same time of the perception's being unchanged.
[4] Do not ask yourself "How does it work with me?" Ask "What do I know about someone else?"
[5] Here it is useful to introduce the idea of a picture-object.
[6] A child can talk to picture-men or picture-animals. It can treat them as it treats dolls.
[7] Hence the flashing of an aspect on us seems half visual experience, half thought.

ZETTEL

Sure
if we are to speak of the experience of thinking
the experience of speaking is as good as any,
thus:
"Who is Wittgenstein?"
                      (she said, having been present
                      at some months' acrimonious
                      debate on *Philosophical Investigations*)
With the configuration of chess-pieces
limbs describe themselves in rooms
under the angle-poise.
"What is the opposite of brown?
—orange?
—another shade
of brown."
Limbs of the angle alter,
poise, in rooms:
what is the opposite of me?
—you?
—another shade
of me.
Suppose it were
part of my day-dream to say
"I am merely engaged in fantasy."
I can write
"I am healthy."
in the dialogue of a play
and so not mean it,
although it is true.
This is dialogue in a play
—the language-game
with pronouns.
A spot-light swivels
through faces of the cast and rests in
the mirror.

One can own a mirror
does one then own the reflections
that may be seen in it?
I love you.
—the language-game
with pronouns and
"Confucius he say":
The concept of a living being
has the same indeterminacy
as that of a language.
Love is not a feeling.
Love is put to the test
—the *grammatical* test.

Anyone who does not understand
why we talk about these things
must feel what we say to be mere trifling,
thus:
"It seems a bit of a fuss about nothing."
                              (she said after reading
                              The Language of Criticism)
Roomspace in which we dispose
ourselves is not external.
The gap between
my purple trousers
and his pale-green shirt
is then
grammatical.
I love you.
One says the ordinary thing
—with the wrong gesture.
Folded & re
folded the
map of the
town is pass
ed through

our lives
& hands ac
ross the table.

The *same* indeterminacy though,
which could suggest a cast-
list drawn up in language
play, that speech commits
to fantasy. And so it does
at least in the first
person singular, for:
One's hand writes
it does not write because one wills
but one wills
what it writes.

(Quotations from Wittgenstein, Zettel.*)*

ACROSTIC

And can the first attitude of all
be directed towards a possible disillusion
so that one learns from the beginning,
"That is probably a chair."
Thys crede is called Simbolum
that is to say a gatherynge of morselles.
Choice of words is the best paradigm
for other choices. What other choices?
I have as many friends as the number
yielded by the solution of this
equation. For the college system
makes "pretty inchoate" a topic—
itself—of the present dissertation.

And now how does one learn the question?
"Is it also really a chair?" Well
bit by bit daily life becomes such
that there is a place for hope in it.
The name begins to mean its bearer.
(A connection between the concept
of meaning and the concept of teaching.)
Is someone speaking untruth?
If I say "I am not conscious."
"I am not in love any more."
And suppose a parrot says:
"I don't understand a word."
or a gramophone: "I am only
a machine." I am only
a machine and paint my love
by numbers, a gathering of morsels.
For the meaning of a name
is not its bearer. (And truth
if I say it while unconscious)
I like things this way.
They are probably, chairs?

(Quotations from Zettel.*)*

IDOLS OF THE (SUPER)MARKET

"Wittgenstein would say"
                    (L.W. 1889–1951)
but he is dead;
therefore and nevertheless
can be said in literary monograph to say
anything.
No more helpless in this respect
than we, the stakes in our own
language-games—Eng. Lit. in this case
but History or Science
will serve the purpose equally well.
"Perfection of the life or of the work."
                    (W.B.Y. 1865–1939)
"Perfection is possible in neither."
                    (W.H.A. 1907–   )
These are some of the
Lessons of the Masters
                    (and another is that sexuality
                    is a branch of aesthetics;
                    but that really is a digression.)
Further both meanings
of hieros
          (Gk. sacred, accursed)
apply to the Sacred Fount, "from
whence my being flows
or else dries up."
                    (H.J. 1843–1916
                    W.S. 1564–1616)
Minny Temple dies for him.
He found it necessary for red hair
to become pigment on a canvas
by Bronzino. It is necessary
for us to become pigment
and when confronted, on any
social occasion, with the canvas

                                        (in the art of the novel
                                        there is no scene
                                        that is not plot,
                                        no dialogue
                                        that is not scene.)
to say, as of Wittgenstein,
"and dead, dead, dead."
But "art is disposable nowadays"
which makes the definition that much
more difficult; especially as a
psychiatric hospital sifts more
efficiently "the mad abstract dark."

(or else dries up)

ANTIPHRASIS

I went to the British Museum
I looked at the Egyptian Antiquities;
neat syntax of ibis and scarab
sum up my several identities;
the stone face is dumb,
the mummy enclosed in its chattering sarcophagus.
I stared at the Rosetta Stone
I was irritated by a crowd of French schoolchildren
My feet hurt.
I am working at the collation
of these parallel texts
"the t'one in ye proper simple speech
and t'other by the fygure of irony"
                              (Thos. More, 1533)
Socratic method
(This is to be the theme.)
"esp. in reference to the dissimulation of ignorance
practised by Socrates
                    (c.400 B.C.)
as a means of confounding an adversary."
                              (OED)
Thought is a subversion of reality
and "time is the evil, beloved"
                              (E.P.)
Shall I compare you to Apollo (or Perithoös)
on the west pediment of The Temple of Zeus?
I dreamt you were made of stone
and struck your head off with a pen.
It rolled and lay still and bled
sawdust. There is a sawdust pit
below the sculptures to protect
them from earthquakes which are
frequent in the area. The attribution
of identity (Apollo or Perithoös)
to "you" is disputed.

("Other Minds" etc. vide supra)
Each figurative speech forms
"a contradictory outcome of events
as if in mockery of the promise and fitness of things."
                                                    (*OED*)
I went to the British Museum
I fled from words to stone
I read the chatter of ibis and scarab
on the Egyptian tombs.
"By the fygure *Ironia* which we call the *drye Mock*"
                    (Puttenham, *Arte of English Poesie*, 1589)

ANTIQUITIES

A gesture is adjective,
two hands, granite
when they turn bread to flesh
(Notre Dame, July 14th)
A mirror is a museum-case,
two hands, priestesses'
when she mummifies her face.
Emotion is a parenthesis,
two hands, irony
when I light the candle
and cross myself.
Aesthetic approbation is glass
when it encloses her faience eyes
and gilded skin.
(Musée du Louvre, July 18th)
Glance is the copula
that petrifies our several identities,
syntactic superficies.

II

Michaelmas
My cardboard daisies are in bloom
again.
The city's silhouette stands out
just like real, from a child's
pop-up book, "a castle cut in
paper" (*Gawain & the Grene Knight*
c.1400). Autumn leaves turn like
pages, black on white. For green
and gold must be as parenthetical
as walks through sharpening air
and clamant colour, smoky light
along the Backs, from typewriter
to Library. "Grammar" derives from

"glamour"; ecology may show the two
still cognate: Museum, Gk. mouseion,
a seat of the Muses, a building
dedicated to the pursuit of learning
or the arts. (*OED*)
The glamorous grammatical frames
captions for a monograph on non-
existent plates. Glue, paper,
scissors, and the library together
paste a mock-up of an individual
history. The art of English Poesie?
"Such synne is called yronye."

GROUP THEORY

Certainly
    it is the "cultural level
of a Noah's Ark"
(The animals go in two by two.)
But
    we do inhabit a rainy climate.
And alas
    you can't get a sex change
on the N.H.S.
        Only verbal instruments (Elizabeth Eberhardt
        referred to throughout her diary as "he")
        or linguistic situation (comprising clothes,
        attitudes, behaviour) can perform the delicate
        operation, of altering the terms in an erotic
        equation.
We
    were fitting key
words to our lives
e.g.
Tension, awareness, extremity
(liberté, égalité, fraternité)
She
    hesitated for a long while
then put down her cards;
Michael   amo
    Hamid   amas
        Me   amat
"Of course I know what it means.
I did A level Latin."

Catch phrase
        love all
                    game and set.
There are no
        just(es)
                       mots.

THE HYPHEN
For the centenary of Girton College

i hyphen (Gk. together, in one)
a short dash or line used to connect
two words together as a compound
1869-
1969
to connect Chapel Wing and Library.
But also: to divide
for etymological or other purpose.
A gap in stone makes actual
the paradox of a centenary.
"It was a hyphen connecting different races."
and to the library
"a bridge for migrations".
In search of an etymology
                    for compound lives,
this architecture,
                an exercise in paleography
(Victorian Gothic)
                asserts the same intention.
Portraits busts and books
                the "context in which we occur"
that teaches us our meaning,
                    ignore the lacunae
of a century
            in their state-
ment of our need to hyphenate.

ALKA-SELTZER POEM

With beaded bubbles winking at the brim
the effervescence is subsiding. Drink
before effervescence subsides. Inert
liquid and undissolved tablets are dangerous.
It is like the unperceived rearrangement
of ice, a gradual crackle spreading under
our feet, signalising thaw. In cold weather
Andrew's Liver Salts may be taken in water
with the chill off. Freeze alternatively
or crystallize the alteration in acidic
percentages which is this process of
dissolving. The cause is physiology,
and the effect, metaphor. Alleviation
of the effects of over-indulgence
in alcohol or words is one of her
cloudy trophies. Silver tinsel hangs
like nets of frost, like votive
offerings for our escape from water
in all the shop-windows. "You can use,"
she said, "glue to stick it on with—
Durex." This metaphor requires completion
in a chemists' with a request for a packet
of Durofix (gossamer). For experience
is an active verb and the end
of poetry is activity. Hung-over
this morning in a gossamer net
of words, the bubbles wink & subside.

THREE PROPER

and witte familiar letters
lately passed between two
Universitie men: touching
the Earthquake in April last
and our English reformed
Versifying. (1) Long lackt alas
hath been thy faithful aide in hard essay
Whiles deadly fit thy pupil doth dismay.
I like your late pentameters so exceeding
well that I also enure my Penne sometime
in that kind:
A cuts off
B's arm, shaves
it & sends
it to C,
C being the
logical con
stant, the
situation we
are to infer
from terms
in metaphoric
relation.
We are, for
instance, two
on a raft &
starving, A
a surgeon
with hairless
arms and
ingenuity. Being thus so closely and eagerly
set at our game we scarcely need perceive
the rest: Spanish Burgundy, Georges Brassens,
tripos finished, a lack of love and cigarettes.
P, however, implies Q. The entailment
relation between fact and fiction is perhaps

called metaphor, (B is hirsute and hard-
up.) or some new kind of Cambridge
Platonism:
P cuts off
Q's arm
and puts
it in a
film (a
stocking
stuffed with
handkerchiefs)
sent to X
to the im
mortal mem
ory of Ed
mund Spen
ser (C's
concept of
moral respons
ibility is
exigent.) And V had better mind her p's
and q's. For the entailment works one way
only, poetic licence being allverywellbut.
Sith none that breatheth *living* air
does know where is that happy land of Faëry.
(2) We are all ribosomes
of the same phoneme.
(3) I think the earthquake was also
there with you, overthrowing divers
old buildings and peeces of Churches.
Architecture is the jumping-off point,
for example, The Senate House Leap, to
Caius; it is responsible for a lot. How
oft do they their silver bowers leave
To come to succour us that succour want.
We must admit that the self is not

enclosed by a wall, although castles
of extendible polystyrene may be respons
ible for a lot. A castle is called
Alma. Its
walls are
painted
faire with
memorable
gestes, of
artes, of
science, of
Philosophy
and all that
in the world
was aye thought wittily. *That* hight
Phantastes by its nature true. For when
our minds go wandering uncontrolled, when
we pursue imaginary histories or exercise
our thoughts on some mere supposed
sequence, we give rise to a problem.
Heaven being used shorte as one
sillable when it is in verse.

TWO OTHER

very commendable letters of the same
mens writing: both touching the fore
said Artificial Versifying and certain
other particulars. Enclosed find
my writing up of the W.P.'s M.Phil.
Many thanks for your informed,
intelligent and convivial contribution
to the discussions: The Examination,
to be conducted at 12, Benet Place,
will take the form of an *essay* on
life (No previous knowledge of the
subject will be assumed.) It should
show, within the clear limitations
of the topic, equivalent qualities
of scholarly competence, critical
intelligence and independence of,
thought as required for the Ph.D.
A "high" standard will be maintained.
(It was a convivial contribution.
Whether it nectar or divine tobacco
were, from whence descend all hopeless
remedies.) And yet me thinkes all
should be Gospell that commeth from
you Doctors of Cambridge. Heaven
being used shorte when it is . . .
(Yet verses are not vaine.)
A breaks
down B's
castle &
C rebuilds
it in Ari
zona.
"Architecture
being less
dispensable
than people."
(2) Reason! quoth Madame Incredula.

CRITERIA FOR CONTINUING A SERIES

This is Cambridge
This is Cambridge
The train now standing at Platform 4 terminates
here
will all passengers change
please.

NN. is a *full-time* student
(We are always expecting him to come
to tea; we look at our watches; we
wonder if he smokes.) And Upon
Westminster Bridge, when the light falls
across the green field, he regards the swing
and stillness of the axes of time and place
as lines drawn on the lens of a telescope.
He wonders if this ecstasy is worth
cultivating and "how many" have killed
themselves from "pure joy" (If one is used
to a small river, the Thames is always something
of a shock.) The focus tightens and . . .
rests on the tedium of its metaphor.
It's a mugs game, this stance, after—
Mauberley? NN. is not a mug. This is
to certify that he *is* a full-time student.

Will all passengers change
please?
The focus sharpens and the turning axes
are lying still. Will all passengers terminate
Here?

(We pause a moment; we think; we lay out)
cigarettes.

And for my sixteenth point,
                    Scharazade:
there was a time when
I did *not* want to grow up
because I should have to stop
telling myself stories. But
(were "but" of the stuff)
typing-ribbon at midnight
burns as beautifully as any
Arabian taper.
                    Here we can consult the admirable
                    article de *vulgarisation* de Eccles
                    on the structure of the cerebral cortex.
Yes, I too am slightly tired
of wind-screen wipers. When,
as noted above, the location
of choice implied a technique
for book-binding the universe.
                    I am indebted for this point
                    to my friend, Dante Alighieri.
Now, I get tired of wind-screen
wipers; hence the sun (also) rises.
                    While this was in proof
                    the admirable article appeared.
Furthermore, if you can't say it
                    You can't say it.
and you can't
whistle it
either

"Keep this letter. It is important"

THE FURTHER-OFF-FROM

to Humpty Dumpty, who said
that we could only learn to get the better
of *words*, for the thing which.

And is the oyster also the pearl,
then what about the oyster
                                    catcher

(The walrus and the carpenter were sitting in a pub.
Said the walrus to the carpenter: Aye there's the rub.
If I'd had your opportunities you wouldn't now catch me
Gulping down the oysters and swilling the Chablis.
Deep I should go diving in an image of the sea.)

How high they flow here, butter
and tears that is, everything, that is,
2.3*d* for a packet of
                                    crumpets, the

(Said carpenter to walrus: I speak of course, professionally
And I charge for my aqua-lung a nominal fee.
The gap between oyster and pearl as you know,
Is a matter for Linguistics. Skål, Malvolio!
We're not sick yet of self-love, or even L.W.)

world. If the catcher opened the oyster
would he "deeply sympathise", would he see
it was thinking of what
                                    pearl

(Nothing but: Cut us another slice.)

PHRASE-BOOK

Words are a monstrous excrescence.
Everything green is extended. It
is apricot, orange, lemon, olive and cherry,
and other snakes in the linguistic grass;
also a white touch of marble which evokes
no ghosts, the taste of squid, the . . .
Go away. I shall call a policeman.
Acrocorinth which evokes no
goats under the lemon blossom.

World is a monstrous excrescence;
he is following me everywhere, one
Nescafé and twenty Athenes, everything
green; I am not responsible for it.
I don't want to speak to you.
Leave me alone. I shall stay here.
I refuse a green extension. Beware.
I have paid you. I have paid you
enough, sea, sun, and octopodi.
It is raining cats and allomorphs.

"Where" is the British Embassy.

A FORTIORI

their fractured grace: the wind
disintegrates raindrops: the raindrops
dissolve, a metal grid, that falls.

If all meaning is diacritical, one
will see dualism in anything intelligible.

The eye is like Aprile, that falleth, a priori,
on the flower, the grass, the bird,
the fire-escape—its frame shifted by drops

that glance, with their bright eye-balls
fractured in the wind: the blank world
which its whiteness defends.

All dualisms are not equivalent
nor do they imply one another.

Whiteness defends the grass, the bird, the
raindrops, a light that falls refracts
our fractured grace: our glance: the wind.

IT DOESN'T MATTER ABOUT MANTRIPPE

his is an uncommon name, uncited in linguistic
examples. It is not he
        who kissed the girl who lives in college
        was surprised to find himself supervised by George
        could not have thought that Newton *is* considered
        the greatest English physicist, exhibited
        a tough reasonableness beneath his slight lyric grace.
He is going into the F.O. and will not be required
for linguistic examples. Reading about Politics
will not help him to pass the Moral, Science, Tripos.
He wouldn't put it this way; in fact he did
put it this way: "I thought Newton is considered
the greatest English beach-comber."

           "Yes I saw two
ducks the other day." "My 'o's have changed this year."
"Il était d'un air terrible, affreusement consterné."
"Are party conversations like this in Politics?"
The pebbles slide through our fingers, worry
beads brought back from Greece as souvenir and
conversation peace; and we are surprised sometimes
to find that we could not have kissed the girl who
lives in college, that Politics *is* a great ocean
of undiscovered linguistic examples, that we
are Mantrippe's supervisor.

           I lay in bed, fishing
with the Alka-Seltzer glass beside me. Brother
Urusov came and we talked about the vanity
of the world; there was nothing to say after,
he had pointed out Battersea Power Station.
People who were here before Wittgenstein came
still have command of their "Faculties".
There are no unacceptable sentences, only
impossible worlds; Einstein *has* visited
Troy; we *have* filled our mouths with worry, beads
and it doesn't
        matter
           about
              Mantrippe.

On the Periphery

(1975)

the:
the mentioning—run
ubiquitous, Victorian, similar
chism.
Shall topoi, conventional
—momentarily—
elaboration?

Had they conceits?

IN DEFENCE OF GRAHAM HOUGH: STYLE AND STYLISTICS

Study Linguistics
            to texture received: reader
                            unity
                            literary

Literary General
            to impression: strivings, as—
                            the language
                            kind
                            technical
                            imagery

Different is a close: the
"of we literary"

cannot of
        —of time subjective—
against the
        —the that

                limited?

These three pieces are aleatory poems. They were constructed by noting the last word on the top left-hand corner of consecutive pages in, respectively, *The Common Pursuit* by F.R. Leavis, *Style and Stylistics* by Graham Hough, and Kant's *Critique of Judgement*. The words thus obtained were then arranged as juxtapositions of contexts from which, by following certain conventions of poetic reading, meaning could be obtained. The justification of this enterprise is the fuller knowledge thereby gained of all our processes of understanding—especially—very contemporary poetic techniques. And for this reason they are placed at the beginning of this book.

TO R.Z. AND M.W.

the figure of
               our two friends in
the darkness of
               our familiar city
walking with
               their arms around
each other
               "perhaps"

how is *this*
               relationship "going":
between
               two friends &
the figure:
               the familiar city of
each other
               walking.

ON NAMING OF SHADOWS

Thus the morning's shadow of
    a pigeon's wing
became pretext for each darkness
    in the day,
for the naming of wings &
    moths and move-
ment of leaves, justified each
    by its shade.

I have actually just two
    elements, platinum &
chromium, also some uninterpreted
    spectra, a box
of them, lying around, more
    than I can
fit into a formulated crystal
    the colour of

leaves (green) pigeons (multi) moths
    etc. It is
a jump of several orders of magni-
    tude from shade
to this: a ray of light
    entering a
tourmaline, split up in
    two ways

one, the ordinary, perpendicular
    the other,
extraordinary, parallel, vibrates
    to the prin-
cipal axis of a bifurcated
    obsession.
Its general appearance (the stone)
    colourless &

clear, or black & opaque; but
    (the jump)
also various shades of brown
    red, yellow
green, blue, banded hues where
    we deal
not with absorption, but emission, for there
    is visible, light.

SELECTION RESTRICTIONS ON PEANUTS FOR DINNER

Tenacity was sticking to the topic
        of blankets
and walnuts, French: noix
           noisette: a hazel nut.
One word can include two unities;
           the difficulty
is to recognise when this is the case:
            a little nut; or take
blankets: the weave of two senses
          under them
makes nothing of six-term dinner
          table textures
but do they, even securely tucked
          at the corners,
comprehend a unity?

            Sweat is not more impure
than tears;
      and indeed it is often followed by them.
The words
      were too hot for blankets
or unity.
      An acorn developed into every oak.

FOR THE SPIDER WHO FREQUENTS OUR BATH

First there is secure, scuttling
                                    in the rustic darkness (
the waste-pipe, no
                    Freudian repository)
which lacks only a corner
                            to hang a web on.

But the end is enamelled
                            allegory; its dazzle (
a white field for
                    Chaucerian spring)
which coloured globes of
                            Bubble-Bath do not evade.

L'EFFET DU RÉEL

We like watching the sea going away from us
and also retreating certain promises the sky held:
of breaking waves.
Now, this is the regular "Norman landscape";
mist rises through straight-planted trees.
We like watching the road going away from us
in ripples yellow like "specks of foam"
and also retreating certain by-roads from this fracture
of events.
We construct an event out of, behind these shutters "people"
are sleeping.
and from an intersection between "the most perfect château of the
        transition period"
and "a cricket on a ball of dung". Our capacity
for indifference is truly astounding

Until the rock
will turn to
air at a ruin-
ed tower
& we step
over its sill
the doors &
sills of light.

So would you mind just standing in the café doorway
for a minute longer against the sun because I'm
writing a poem about intersections (the doors & sills of light)
between the mind and stone, imagination and reality; and because
everything's fine for my palms drip sweat and all the leg muscles
tremble so nicely in the unconstructed event of such a journey.

We do not watch with complacency the sea retreating, leaving
the stonework stranded in its imaginary light like
your shadow in the café door. So again laughter muscles
go through their contractions nicely, for it's all right;
you can move now. Such savage triumph returns us to Maillezais.
The abbey stands still, without quotation marks.

AN ARBITRARY LEAF

Printed in natural colours, we find a way always
to deny the world; even its "aerial view" from
"the tower itself". A biro-cross marks the place
where our arcades and buttresses dissolved in air;
but still it is a "carte-postale de luxe" bought as
reminder of an "extraordinary experience".
These occasions have a way of multiplying.
The treads uneven, between steps with "five-hundred years of wear";
and darkened to an height of—wouldn't you say—
about the same number of feet. This would never be allowed
in England: such sudden and insouciant lack
of the next step. Give me your hand.

Shall we exorcise the colours that contrast us
with the evening walk? Any next walk must be this one,
now that we have given it the article, consciously
evoked in word and gesture: our shadowy design to
undermine the objects on our path.
So that this dead leaf, in lack of colour and
perfected shape is like fan-vaulting discerned
in the abbey—communication having been accepted—
But no finality in such a text can justify
a reference to Clément and his castle, Villandraut.

PFARR-SCHMERZ (VILLAGE-ANGUISH)

Making love & omelettes
                    For every poem ought to contain
                    at least one zeugma
we may discern a very
palpable corner of a
sheet. Like love it
                    It ought to; and since "is"
                    may be derived from "ought",
                    the sheet, the situation and
                    ourselves exist (see, *Proc. Arist. Soc.*,
                    supp. vol. XCCCI)
is like the palpable
light set square
in wooden tapestry
                    stained glass (see La Sainte Chapelle)
like irony discerned
in fan-vaulting.
Interlocking rings
of glazed perception
turn in our eyes &
fingers, to be unravelled, Chinese
                    It was, therefore, quite right
                    of Chiang Hen to write down
                    the text only. For if the student
                    concentrates and uses his mind
                    he will discover the process
                    between the lines (see, *The
                    Unwobbling Pivot*, trans. E.P.)
puzzles. Have you
seen the minnows
in the steel-dust,
the rose, the magnet
leaves, in the mere?
                    Irony as an acceptance of limitation
                    is our natural approach to the divine
                    (see, Elizabeth David, *French
                    Provincial Cooking*)

If we are going
to get up we ought
to get up, and
                        Thus we are derived from "ought"
eat our glazed
perceptions in
the form of
croissants, leaving
the palpable corner
to the sheet.

To seek mysteries in the obscure, poking into magic and committing
eccentricities in order to be talked about later—This I do not.

THE DYING GLADIATOR

Di pensier in pensier
from impasse to impasse, from Christmas tree
to jelly-fish, stranded on the sandy bed
of the semiotic sea, his network in the dust;
his vehicle for macroscopic structures,
dismembered by bicycle handlebars
as we crossed King's Parade
                        Did someone speak to me?
From valley to valley;
his eyes upon his native hills, every
marked path hostile to the tranquil life
                        Of reassurance in physical properties
                        like chrysanthemums in a yellow jug
where mist folds knot in nodes
of light, in the multivalence
of an implicated calculus
but *torn* out of our hands
by his entangled fish-spear
                        Like the date on the calendar or
                        a chair for someone I love to sit
                        reading, or a new salad-bowl
from mouth to ashtray
from thread to needle,
from
                        A point of light that reaches through
                        water to the sea-bed where
                        like carnivorous anemones
                        we open
leaning on an elbow
he dies   and close.

DRINKS WITH A MYTHOLOGUE

Le vin est objectivement bon   mais la bonté du vin
est un mythe. The veins are obviously bloodless
but the blood in the veins   is mine. A vision
of ordinary beauty resembles the v in the mind.
The v is obvious in but.   It makes beauty
in verbs a myth. Vacillations of opening blood
burst the beauty of v   that is mine. V
in an ordinary bottle   is the breakdown of verbs
in the mind. Violent   and opening beauty, the bursting
of verbs is a myth. Violence objective and but
is this beauty of   veins in the mind.

"If you smash that glass, my dear, you know
you'll simply have to sweep it up again afterwards.
And anyway it's a waste of good wine!"

ADDRESS TO THE READER, FROM PEVENSEY SLUICE

If it were quicksand you could sink;
something needing a light touch
soon and so simply takes its revenge.
Slightly west of Goodwin Sands
the land hardens again with history,
resists the symbol.
Chalk requires an allegorical hand,
or employee of Sussex Water Board
who sets a notice here:
DANGER SUBMERGED STRUCTURES
and all at once Transformational Grammar
"peoples" the "emotional landscape"
with refutation.
You may hear its melancholy
long withdrawing roar
even on Dover beach watching
the undertow of all those trips
across to France.
Follow the reader and his writer,
those emblematic persons
along their mythic route
charting its uncertain curves and camber;
for to be true to any other you must—
and I shall never now—recover
a popular manœuvre known mostly as,
turn over
and go to sleep.

ON THE PERIPHERY

Ducks flee into the undergrowth
like eponymous heroes as we approach
the past, walking slowly on a path
beside a water-way or something.

These stories are committed to memory
and writing only when they have reached
a high degree of sophistication (we
have reached). Sanctioned and solacing
polythene buttercups strew our way
with images of "natural"
regeneration, inevitable.

Somewhere the table's set far from the traffic
jam, thus she spoke, turning, mov'd
the third heaven, that popular memory.
So many images now set revolving &
oh, that reminds me (poetry functions
as tribal mnemonic) who are we
having for dinner tomorrow.

THE AQUARIUM

Many pills, Matilda, does that make tonight?
But you *must* tell if you take the yellows.
The eyeball, listless under its tiny lid, moves
so slowly that downstairs in the cloakroom
were four rubber boots *all left feet* (this is a
Pedestrian Controlled Crossing but read as you
may you will find no mention of fish) covered even
ly with blood (groping in mud for a sound) whoever
however (and a collision is highly likely to occur)
controls the eyeball ignores this collision and takes
many yellows without telling any; hangs over books
brooding on mud. I, therefore, have nothing to add
to the scene transcribed above and the word that is
murder will fit very well. Over the boots but under
the eyeball are raincoats and hats and quotation
marks all wet through (or with name if you wish
to make plain the pills that we take for our)
into the garden it passes suffused now with pain
like an evening in spring the garland so fresh
and the roses so sweet she gave with intent to perceive.
Freckled by a glance the glass flickering advanc
es away into greenery untouched by the sun. Moreover
the grass also is green, so slowly the eyeball
did turn bloodshot in its emptying socket.

Note: see Roland Barthes: *S/Z, L'Empire des signes*
          Denis Roche: "Leçons sur la vacance poétique" in *Éros énergumène*
          Alain Robbe-Grillet: *La Jalousie*
          and Nathalie Sarraute: *Le Planetarium*

ON READING MR. MELVILLE'S *TALES*

When sunlight wounds me I think of thousands
it has killed on crowded beaches stripped like
knives whetted for sacrificial your hand is on my arm
your lips are on my cheek your eyes are on my eyes
whence water drips theories since Plato strolled
along those shores we have not seen such de
constructed presences of speech and sense so run
the traces through our history like scarlet woven in
a sailor's rope to say it is the King's (is any simile
more inappropriate) generally disseminated like take
O take your hands off me in the civilisation of the West
who ruled the evil and the good (some say that Claggart
is the devil) Shall I be cold and dead my love shall
I unweave the thread but we have superseded such banal
dichotomies as these or shall I join the rest in
holding off the meaning from the form lines present in inter
textual strands I should not like to hang despite Platon
Like Billy Budd my heart would stop; it has stopped;
the differment remains, remains and

Note: see Herman Melville: "Billy Budd, Sailor, an inside narrative"
Jacques Derrida: "L'Écriture et la différence" and
De la grammatologie
Julia Kristeva: *Semiotike: Recherches pour une sémanalyse*
and William Empson: "Missing Dates", *passim.*

APPROACHING THE LIBRARY

You never would have believed it could be so easy;
it played into one's hands, the unpremeditate paysage,
as Stevens said, crossing the fen, suddenly confronted
with such expanse of unpretentious waters as visit
our dreams. Elle resta, comme le dit Flaubert,
melancholique devant son rêve accompli.

Poetic diction performed for me two outstanding services:
in confirming that the subject I proposed treating
was a worthy one; and in feeding and clothing me
after I had, in a moment of abstraction, fallen
into Holme Fen Engine Ditch;

It partakes of the clay's history of human blood
and strife, like Devil's Dyke, our excursion to which
is hereby premeditated. Thus we are rescued from
the abstract ditch we dig with our fundamental
disagreement about the proper form for a picnic.

It is disturbing to find oneself on a level
with the river, smooth-flowing with pronouns
where we grub, like ducks, for whatever they eat,
in unexpected pools. A drastic diminution
of pronouns in the early weeks of marriage
(lack of third persons, not to mention more banal examples)
leads to this retracted meadow in which comparisons
must be deployed, the meadow she crosses now,
noting its blossoming synecdoches, on her way
to the library, carrying her *Heffers Cantab Students
Notebook, ref. 140, punched for filing.*

LEAVING THE LIBRARY

These daffodils are piston-rods which turn
faster and faster carrying (me). Insomnia
results from coffee and stimulating
company. Toilet rolls oscillate wildly
in all the cubicles as the train gathers
speed, etc. And so much for that image.
Exuberant pronouns flourish like baroque
cherubs in the spring air beckoning.
It would be possible to contact the
"actual world" if they flourished more
like the threatening anonymity of real
children, stumbled over in a street.
But this grace is denied (me).
Shoulder your skis or your umbrella and
glide with the pronouns over the bridge
past daffodils thumping like your
insomniac's heart, your shopping bag
is filled with the week's supply of
toilet rolls, which is a kind of integr-
ation between the image and reality.

FACSIMILE OF A WASTE LAND

And if Another knows I have a little nut-tree cultivated indoors
I know that in this climate nothing will it bear
despite much watering with sighs and tears.

I know little of horticulture but a silver anguish
supplemented by sundry domestic details not Christmas tinselled
and a golden fear of succumbing to the violet typing-ribbon,

Who only know that in return for the kiss you gave to me,
not here, O, Adeimantus, but in another world,
there is no more noise now I hand you the fruit of

More than a year struggling with the violet and the orange peel
which is so alien to my little nut-tree embedded
in the present context of its final version.

Note: the lines:
        "And if Another knows I know I know not
        Who only know that there is no more noise now"
        were omitted by Eliot from his final version, along with:
        "Not here, O, Adeimantus, but in another world".

        Pound was fond of using a violet typewriter ribbon.

PASTORAL

They are our creatures, clover, and they love us
Through the long summer meadows' diesel fumes.
Smooth as their scent and contours clear however
Less than enough to compensate for names.

Jagged are names and not our creatures
Either in kind or movement like the flowers.
Raised voices in a car or by a river
Remind us of the world that is not ours.

Silence in grass and solace in blank verdure
Summon the frightful glare of nouns and nerves.
The gentle foal linguistically wounded
Squeals like a car's brakes
Like our twisted words.

NOT PASTORAL ENOUGH
homage to William Empson

It is the sense, it is the sense, controls,
Landing every poem like a fish.
Unhuman forms must not assert their roles.

Glittering scales require the deadly tolls
Of net and knife. Scales fall to relish.
It is the sense, it is the sense, controls.

Yet languages are apt to miss on souls
If reason only guts them. Applying the wish,
Unhuman forms must not assert their roles,

Ignores the fact that poems have two poles
That must be opposite. Hard then to finish
It is the sense, it is the sense, controls,

Without a sense of lining up for doles
From other kitchens that give us the garnish:
Unhuman forms must not assert their roles.

And this (forgive me) is like carrying coals
To Sheffield. Irrelevance betrays a formal anguish.
It is the sense, it is the sense, controls,
"Unhuman forms must not assert their roles".

LE SIGNE (CYGNE)

Godard, the anthropological swan
floats on the Cam when day is done.
Lévi-Strauss stands on a bridge and calls:
Birds love freedom; they build themselves homes;
They often engage in human relations.
Come Godard, come, here, Godard, here. The halls
of Clare and Trinity, John's and Queens'
echo the sound with scraping of chairs
and cramming of maws. A red-gowned don
floats by the swan. We must try to explain
to the posturing dancers that this is an image
of human existence; this is the barre-work
of verbal behaviour; this knife in the corpse
that they shove through a window to float
down the Cam when day is done
is Godard, the anthropological swan.

CONVERSATION ON A BENIN HEAD

You must come to terms with T.S. Eliot
If you are doing the twentieth-century.
At Girton my gloves and my heart under
My gloves. Words as they chanceably fall
From the mouth change colour whatever
The source, pages or brain or midway
Between window and chair. These colours,
Brown wood air grey ink black, we didn't
Create them. We don't believe they are there
Whatever they are or this is a dagger.
We *know* it's a dagger or nothing whatever:
A scream, a sentence, a phantom, a reading
Of Laing. Believe that my neck is supported
By circuits of communication, gold rings,
I know that and hundred in number, remember
Believe that my throat will collapse; flat
Nose and fat lips disintegrate quickly under
Your touch. Listen. I know it's a dagger.

Whatever it was I didn't do it.

A man must do something. If one
Thinks of other however the chances
Of seeming to cover a single event,
Not in the mind of the doer, the point
Of departure is hard to recover. It all
Goes to clothes and the moves
Of the wearer infinite in number
Between window and bed and he
Turned as he said it all goes to show
You have never been whether
Reluctant to swallow the trace of another
Or touch at your own. We'll collect
Them tomorrow. Such monuments over
The gathering quick of your pink
Little finger furrowing under the bone
Of my skull. Own this armour at least,
This stylistic skeleton caught in the last arabesque

but one.

THE EAR OF DIONYSIOS: ODE
for Linda Sparkes

Below the Greek amphitheatre
on the left of the Roman stadium
beyond the cord-makers grotto,
the monument thus named is found
to be one of the greatest engineering feats
of the ancient world. It was designed
for Dionysios, tyrant of Syracuse,
as a dungeon whence his prisoners' voices
would reach 1000 ft to his own less
permanent tympanum. If the tourist
will try the experiment he may hear
his own words echo throughout the
vast moist aperture. But Dionysios doesn't
listen any more. Je suis la victime et le bureau.

You are not like me; you are Giselle, Odette in this world of
similar asparagus (and no crummy puns on corps de ballet from
the audience; take your filthy words off her) or a waitress with
a Cockney accent. You are not like me; you are me in any of
these roles and your hair is not golden but brown if I want it to
be, and your body, mine in the bath.

All eras of decadence are as similar as asparagus; and I intend no
reference to Dowson's paidophilia, Swinburne's algolagnia or
Symons' cabaret dancers. These are monetary transactions
scented with white heliotrope.

Still white heliotrope
                    topic of still waters which run deep
when you are rowing
                    towing a growing sense of fear of
tropes in the boat.
                    You can't return to the other shore
for it is before
                    you rowed roamed and jumped
into the tangled isles.
                    We are getting over-heated

and a second driver is risky
                    nevertheless refill the flask in Loch Ness
despite no road on the other shore.
                    And mother rows
over the scent in the bath.
                    It was a steep descent, helio
was nothing to it.
                    Stagnant waters run deep and half and
you had better let me steer clear, dear
                                    though I am ignorant of
                                            sailing and
the steering veers
                    from shore to shore, I can give you
metaphor for metaphor
                    any day and get away along the
coastline of literary peaks
                    and threatening summits (Ben Ezra etc.—
                                    my crummy puns)

            In places the mask slips the man shows clear
            with his bigotry hatred and fear;
            and in others his passionate tender heart?
            No, I fear art's a hard thing, my dear,
            there one sees just the greatness of art.

and plant their superfluous road-signs
                                    long before for it is before
as aforesaid and "who
                    are you anyway" said Mr. Ashbery before
who *lives* in New York
                    (another 1400 ft peak)
if you are mother or the other
                                    I can offer you no hope
therefore perhaps however you are:

The dancer who is avatar with golden hair
of everyone who has been lost. Should I not share
her weary elbow on the barre. Rossetti
might have gestured thus. He named her this.
Yesterday she lost her bra. Some fetishists
are more banal than I who envy tears and sweat
for bleeding toes in satin shoes, enchainment
(Yeats') from mind to tree, but can't leap out of irony.
That they keep grace with such as she.

an estimated 75% of Chinese restaurants
in Paris are used as cover for spies. De spies.
Replies to official questions were various,
ranging from "we used to have some spies but
they left; they didn't say where they were going;
every restaurant has its ups and downs"
to "sorry, no spies, but very good Peking duck".

Je suis la victime et le bureau.

Memorial to the deportation. Whose? Jews. Yours. Ours. I consider
this an insult to my staff about whom I am most particular; there
are no spies here; anyway spies don't exist.
White blocks   black lines stone by   steel grille   by grille   line by
line across the white and black block of the page.
There has been a new edition true to the new edition. (No God but
confusion and Pound is its prophet; it floats on the sterling market.
I smell a rat; I see it floating through the air; but I shall nip it in the
bud. Ring-ring-a-roses, all fall down.) There has been a new edition
of L'Histoire de la folie which costs too much; and in order to change
your traveller's cheques you must return whence you came
(a bench in the Luxembourg gardens) and know the place for the
first time. Deconstruction
costs too much; le silence des siècles m'envahit; Le tourbillonnement
des siècles m'envahit. Il n'y a rien à te faire peur dès que tu monte
ou que tu descend la tour de Notre Dame de Chartres. Montez-
vous ou descendez-vous? She has a lightning-conductor on her
back and from the tower you can see into the men's urinal (and
know the place for the first time). I've never known what this fish
was called in English, lieu: plaice? This is in memory of Max Jacob,
paysan de Paris à paraître. Apparaîtra le pari et paresse d'être de la
vie. La paresse des siècles m'envahit avec son révolver à cheveux
blancs: animula vagula blandula   hospes comesque corporis   quae
nunc abibis in loca   pallidula rigida nudula   nec ut soles dabis
iocos. Facilis decensus Averno, this commemoration. But even
Breton refrained from firing the revolutionary revolver. Revolving

of revolution makes a priest always available; and you can teach its
candles to burn bright. Facilis decensus Averno in deportation in
memory of Max Jacob. Rest in peace with the priest of revolution.
Quos nunc abibis in locos? Les billets ne sont plus valables au
Luxembourg.
If I think of a king at star-fall Ἀστὴρ πρὶν μὲν ἔλαμπες ἐνὶ
ζωοῖσιν Ἑῷος

IN MEMORIAM EZRA POUND
obit first November
nineteen seventy two

Transpontine Ovid made his ovoid obsequies
unto the only emperor, the emperor of ice-cream.
In his elegies Teddy Bear is having picnics.
Can you find four ice-cream cornets hidden
in this elegiac picture? I pasture the pastel
colours of the heart, a part from and partial sense
of lethal elegies hidden in the provinces
of desolation and ice-cream, "the lost land
of Childhood", and the defeated past. Eyes
of a sleeper waked from fantasies (and this
is something more than fantasy) stance of a suicide
above the precipice of emptiness knowing that it must fill:
the fingers find the eyes and type. Take down the book.

Sometimes I think that this is the only thing, the
only stance, first slurp of ice-cream down the throat,
what Krishna meant as when he admonished Arjuna
on the field of battle. Pluck the petal
in the orchard where the factions act on emblematic
colours, red and white; leap with Nijinsky always
poised for entrance in *Le Spectre de la rose.* This
spectred isle, defying death with gesture. Awhile
to porpoise pause and smile and leap into the past.

He is not here he has outsoared the shadow
of our right. 'Tis life is dead not he. And
ghastly through the drivelling ghosts on the bald
street breaks the blank day of critical interpretation
staining the white radiance of eternity, every
little pimple had a tear in it, a fear of many
coloured glass, the noise of life strains the white
radiance of an elegy. How does the stress fall
on an autumn day. Remember remember the first
of November where history is here and nowhere:
the room in Poictiers where no shadow falls

on the pattern of timeless moments. Forget
the gate of white is the gate wherein our past
is laid. These books are radiant as time
against the shadow of our night where no
shadow falls. He is not dead.   Instead.

Give back my swing. O Ferris wheel.

STRIKE
for Bonnie, my first horse

I

Hail to thee, blithe horse, bird thou never wert!
And, breaking into a canter, I set off on the long road south
Which was to take me to so many strange places,
That room in Cambridge, that room in Cambridge, that room in
    Cambridge,
That room in Cambridge, this room in Cambridge,
The top of a castle in Provence and an aeroplane in mid-Atlantic.
Strange people, that lover, that lover, that lover, that lover.
Eyes that last I saw in lecture-rooms
Or in the Reading Room of The British Museum reading, writing,
Reeling, writhing, and typing all night (it's cheaper than getting
    drunk),
Doing tour en diagonale in ballet class (that's cheaper than getting
    drunk too).
But first I should describe my mount. His strange colour;
He was lilac with deep purple points (he was really a siamese cat).
His strange toss and whinny which turned my stomach
And nearly threw me out of the saddle. His eyes
His eyes his eyes his eyes his eyes
Eyes that last I saw in lecture rooms
His eyes were hazel brown and deceptively disingenuous.
I got to know those eyes very well.
Our journey through England was not made easier by the fact
That he would eat only strawberries and cream (at any season).
And he wanted a lot of that.
Nevertheless I got here and the first time I ever set foot in the place
I knew it was my home. The trouble was to convince the authorities.
Jobs were scarce and someone with a purple-point siamese to keep
In strawberries and cream has a certain standard of living.
When I sold my rings and stopped buying clothes I knew
It was the end. When I cut down on food it was clear
I was on some sort of quest.
There was an I-have-been-here-before kind of feeling about it.
That hateful cripple with the twisted grin. But
Dauntless the slughorn to my ear I set.

II
How many miles to Babylon?
Threescore and ten.
Can I get there by candlelight?
Yes. But back again?
From perfect leaf there need not be
Petals or even rosemary.
One thing then burnt rests on the tree:
The woodspurge has a cup of three,
One for you, and one for me,
And one for the one we cannot see.

III
What there is now to celebrate:
The only art where failure is renowned.
A local loss
Across and off the platform-ticket found
For the one journey we can tolerate:
To withered fantasy
From stale reality. Father, I cannot tell a lie;
I haven't got the time.
Mirth cannot move a soul in agony.
Stainless steel sintered and disowned;
Stars in the brittle distance just on loan.
The timetables of our anxiety glitter, grow
One in the alone. The cosmic ozones know
Our lease is running out.
Deserted now the house of fiction stands
Exams within and driving tests without,
Shading the purpose from the promised lands
No milk our honey.
And the train we catch can't take us yet
To the blind corner where he waits
Between the milk and honey gates:
The god we have not met.

THE LADY OF SHALOTT: ODE

The child in the snow has found her mouth,
And estate-agents must beware;
For if what we are seeking is not the truth
And we've only a lie to share,
The modern conveniences won't last out,
Bear tear flair dare,
And the old ones just don't care.

Back and forth she moves her arms;
Forth and back, her legs.
No one would care to say:
Her lips are red, her looks are free,
Her locks are yellow as gold,
Whether she's very young or old,
The nightmare life-in-death is she,
Who thicks men's blood with cold.

What of the future is in the past
Channels towards us now.
Present and future perfect past
Makes no tracks in the snow.
Turn the tap and water will come
For five seconds
And then the sand
Flows into our ever-open mouth.
What was it we understand?

She does not stand in the snow; she kneels:
A parody of prayer.
Lucretius said it long ago:
Why think the gods care?
When the telephone goes dead,
The fridge is broken, the light . . .

Why should we think of knowledge as light;
There is enough to see her.
And, having seen, the message is plain
To those who wish to know
(They are not many):
Run quickly back to darkness again;
We have seen the child in the snow.

THE GARDEN OF PROSERPINE

Th'expence of spirit in a waste of shame
Is lust in action and, till action, lust
Until my last lost taper's end be spent
My sick taper does begin to wink
And, O, many-toned, immortal Aphrodite,
Lend me thy girdle.
You can spare it for an hour or so
Until Zeus has got back his erection.

Here where all trouble seems
Dead winds' and spent waves' riot
In doubtful dreams of dreams.
The moon is sinking, and the Pleiades,
Mid Night; and time runs on she said.
I lie alone. I am aweary, aweary,
I would that I were dead.
Be my partner and you'll never regret it.
Gods and poets ought to stick together;
They make a strong combination.
So just make him love me again,
You good old triple goddess of tight corners.
And leave me to deal with gloomy Dis.

Death never seems a particularly informative topic for poets
Though that doesn't stop them dilating at length upon it.
But then they would dilate on anything.
Love, on the other hand, however trite, is always interesting
At least to those in its clutches
And usually also to their readers.
For, even if the readers be not in its clutches
They think they would like to be
Because they think it is a pleasant experience.
I, however, know better.
And so do Sappho, Shakespeare, Swinburne, Tennyson and Eliot.
Not to mention the Greek dramatists:
Sophocles, Euripedes, Aeschylos, and Eliot.
We all know better.

Love is hellish.
Which is why Aphrodite is also Persephone,
Queen of love and death.
Love kills people and the police can't do anything to stop it.
Love will:
> ravage your beauty
> disrupt your career
> break up your friendships
> squander your energy
> spend every last drop of your self-possession

Even supposing you had such qualities to start with.
The god knows why we bother with it.
It is because it bothers with us.
It won't leave us alone for a minute.
For without us it wouldn't exist.
And that is the secret of all human preoccupation
(As others have said before me)
Love, death, time, beauty, the whole bag of tricks.
All our own work including, of course, the gods.
And we let them ride us like the fools we are.
Of all follies that is the penultimate:
To let our own inventions destroy us,
The ultimate folly, of course, is not to let them destroy us.
To pretend a stoic indifference, mask merely of stupidity.
To become ascetic, superior to the pure pleasures of the senses,
Arrogant and imbecile senecans, unconscious
Of what is going on even in their own bodies
Old whatsisname stuck up on his pillar,
A laughing stock, the ultimate in insensitivity.

The only thing, contrarily, to do with the problem of love—
As with all other problems—
Is to try to solve it.
You won't succeed but you won't make a fool of yourself, trying
Or, at least, not so much of a fool as those who refuse to try.
So here we go for another trip and hold onto your seat-belt,
> Persephone.

I loved you and you loved me
And then we made a mess.
We still loved each other but
We loved each other less.

I got a job, I wrote a book,
I turned again to play.
However I found out by then
That you had gone away.

My dignity dictated
A restrained farewell.
But I love you so much
Dignity can go to hell.

I went to hell with dignity,
For by then, we were three.
And whatever I feel about you,
I certainly hate she.

The god knows what will be the end
And he will never tell.
For I love you and you love me
Although we are in hell.

And what death has to do with it
Is always simply this:
If it isn't your arms I'm heading for
It's the arms of gloomy Dis.

SONNET

My love, if I write a song for you
To that extent you are gone
For, as everyone says, and I know it's true:
We are all always alone.

Never so separate trying to be two
And the busy old fool is right.
To try and finger myself from you
Distinguishes day from night.

If I say "I love you" we can't but laugh
Since irony knows what we'll say.
If I try to free myself by my craft
You vary as night from day.

So, accept the wish for the deed my dear.
Words were made to prevent us near.

Further Poems

A PLEA FOR EXCUSES
i.m. J.L. Austin

The clue discovered in a *performative*
verb promises completion to the poem;
it defines "the indirect free style"
by which narrators indicate these thoughts
are not of them, but of their creatures.

Free, that is, to impute our contingencies
to words, our creatures; indirect that
"is", since the object in parenthesis
is only "to be" experienced; and style?
well, this subject is to many a *nominal*

unhappiness, especially, articulate insincerity;
which let us avoid, creating for an object
the parenthetical excuse, and for a subject,
logical form:
        if . . . (the cat is on the mat)
      and if . . . (it is not the case that the cat is on the mat)
        then . . . (all possible worlds exist)

        if . . . (world is language)
      and if . . . (it is not the case that world is language)
        then . . . (all possible words are true)

Thus: all possible words exist and we are true
to none, unless the poem be performative
and promises that we exist (We promise
that it is.)
        There may be pleasure equally
In deploying the ambiguous richness
of unhappy words, and

          in   (placing
          the   delicate wrist
    against the   formica table-edge
        and   watching
        the   fingers
                            tremble.)

[1]The poet begins his story as he later ends it,
by placing Arthur's reign in historical perspective.
In one hand he holds a Christmas Tree
that is goodliest in green when groves are bare.
First the translation must preserve
the formulaic character of language:
disentangle invention from imitation.
An axe is not like a knife that carves a turkey.
If there be one so wilful my words to assay
let him leap lightly hither, lay hold of this weapon,
I quitclaim it forever; cranberry sauce is not like blood.
Our snowman is seen out of the window, in candlelight;
he is not a symbol of artifice.
Now let's make some plausible definitions, for example;
Beheading Game: the Dictionary Game, any reiterated
temptation to sever; Snowman: a symbol of artifice,
a kind of ceremonial boomerang; Getting Drunk
on Christmas Night: a wicked work, in words to expound.
We agreed to accept each other's pentangle;
this is called, The Exchange of Winnings.
For it is a figure formed of five points
to be token of truth, like laying the table.

THE TEMPTATION

I should have thought you: a squirrel,
hunted from a bird-table by images:
tokens of a non-verbal world, green
knights, rhyme schemes, Morgan le Fay:
signals with flashing lights for eyes
in the cut heads they hold towards you:
mouths full of adjectives and similes.
You would have claimed a kiss by your courtesy,
through some touch or trick of phrase
at some tale's end. You arranged:

the bedroom scene, the woodland scene,
the winter journey, the set table.
I should have held the mirror
for you to adjust your grammar.
At least accept this scrap of green silk,
as a protection from cranberry sauce
and other poetic analogies,
if you be Gawain, which I begin to doubt.

THE EXCHANGE OF WINNINGS

"Will you have some more white meat?"

I have a little hour-glass

I have a little hour-glass
Nothing will it give
But the trickling sound of
Water through a sieve.

All the bright neuroses
Sparkle as they go
Depression and obsession
Back and forth they flow.

Mingled at the bottom
One and one make two
Waiting the reverse, dear,
Quite like me and you.

I have a little nut-tree

I have a little nut-tree
Nothing will it bear
But a silver anguish
And a golden tear.

Now in return for the kiss
You gave to me
I hand you the fruit of
My little nut-tree.

IN MEMORIAM
for W. S. Gilbert

Such is my dream but what am I
An infant crying in the night
An infant crying for the light
And with no language but a cry

That everything should grow divine
If you and I could see and know
The world in one another so
If you were mine.

If you were mine to see and know,
No limit on this world of thine
Be caused by mine,
Except what you would choose to do.

You choose to do what you do show
You take the world away from mine
And make all thine
Hurting me by slow by slow.

Hurting me by slow by slow
When freedom, truth and skill of mine
Could make us great and strong in thine
I know,

The world could be our own I know
If you gave up the hurt of thine
And made life mine.
Apart from you the dark is mine.

Such is my dream; but what am I
An infant crying in the night
An infant crying for the light
And with no language but a cry

Such is my dream but what am I
An old acquaintance of the night,
But I could make all darkness light
If you would try.

CANZON
for British Rail Services

Thou hast committed
fornication

Sols sui qui sai lo sobr'afan qe.m sotz

I know I am not the only to suffer the pains of love.
But this I also know: that each who loves thinks so.
For myself I can only say,
I doubt if any other
Has suffered more than myself
From this overloved desire.

It is always a wrong move
In the chess game of all we do;
It upsets the sparkling play
Whose light desire does smother;
It destroys all kind of breadth
And plunges a quagmire

My self is at one remove
Because it has gone to you
Who will not display
The sense of me another,
Being bound in yourself
By my forlorn desire.

Everything goes to show
That those are lucky who
Keep themselves away
From tangling with another
Cold and in themselves
Unlike my absurd desire.

I desire to love
You and be loved by you
Who cancel out my play
Being so much another
Being so much yourself
Away from my require.

You check my every move
By being what you will do
And not what I could say
To you, my love, an other,
Suffering more myself
By overlove and desire.

And yet I would not not love
If I could chose not to;
For I require to play
By hazarding myself
To you, my self, the other
Whom I always desire.

CODA

                    For
I am Arnaut who drinks the wind
And hunts the hare from the ox
And swims against the stream.

To those who kiss in fear that they shall never kiss again
To those that love with fear that they shall never love again
To such I dedicate this rhyme and what it may contain.
None of us will ever take the transiberian train
Which makes a very satisfactory refrain
Especially as I can repeat it over and over again
Which is the main use of the refrain.

I with no middle flight intend the truth to speak out plain
Of honour truth and love gone by that has come back again
The fact is one grows weary of the love that comes again.
I may not know much about gods but I know that
Eros is a strong purple god.
And that there is a point where incest becomes
Tradition. I don't mean that literally;
I don't love my brother or he me.
We have been mutually avoiding each other
For years and will continue to do so.
Even I know about cross words—
Something. The word you want is Dante.
He said he loved Beatrice. Whatever he did
He didn't love Beatrice. At least the
Beatrice Portinari whom history gives.
He knew her and the point about all these
Florentines is that they all were
Killing each other or dying of rapid
Consumption. Beatrice died; Rossetti painted her
Cutting Dante in the street. Botticelli
Painted the rest: Simonetta Vespucci
Died of a rapid consumption (age 23)
Giuliano dei Medici murdered by the altar rail (age 19)
Guido Cavalcanti died in exile (age 35)
Dante dei Aligeri died in exile (age 90)
Lorenzo dei Medici who lives for ever
Since he stayed there and commissioned

The paintings, and poems and statues
And if he also commissioned the deaths
I don't blame him. He didn't feel
Very magnificent when his brother
Was murdered in sanctuary.
Do you realise whoever did that
Would be excommunicated if, that is, if
He hadn't also murdered the papal legate,
His best friend.
I have lived long enough having seen one thing;
That term has an end.
It was getting dark on the platform of nowhere
When I who was anxious and sad came to you
Out of the rain. Out of the sound of the cold
Wind that blows time before and time after
Even Provence knows.
And as for this line I stole it from T.S. Eliot
And Ezra Pound and A.C. Swinburne. All very good
Poets to steal from since they are all three dead.
The love that is must always just contain
The glory of the love that was whatever be the pain.
We played at mates and mating and stopped up the drain.
Hear me. O Mister Poster I know
You have burnt me too brown you must boil me again
You simply have no notion how delightful it will
Be when they pick us up and throw us with the lobsters out to sea.
It is the lark, my love, and not the nightingale.
None of us will ever take the trans-siberian train.
She wanted to and was collecting people who did
I thought I did but now I know I don't.
It is the lark, my love, and not the nightingale.
In fact I've never heard either bird
But people say they sound very similar.
And what the devil were Romeo and Juliet
About wasting their last moments
Listening to birds. Hah.
I like kicking up larks or
Larking up kicks. So do most poets

Including J.H. Prynne, the memorable poet
Who is happy to say that the U.L.
Has got his middle name wrong.
He claims it stands for Hah
But there is a limit. I know it all.
Riddle me riddle randy ree
Round and round in the snotgreen sea
When they pick us up and throw us
With the Joyces out to sea.
Tell us tale of Troy's downfall
We all would have liked to have been there.
The infernal Odyssos. He it was whose bile
Stirred up by envy and revenge destroyed
The mother of womankind. And Swinburne
Got a kick out of pain but I don't
I just get kicked.
I wish I didn't keep sounding like Richard the Third
Except that if I don't I tend to sound
Like Richard the Second. And who wants that.
I suppose I must sound like Richard the First.
What did he do?
Nothing I take it
I get a kick out of larking up nightingales.
Prynne says that if I don't come back
Safe from Sicily by the thirtieth April
They will send a posse.
March is the cruellest station
Taking on bullying men
And were you really afraid they would rape you?
No. I thought there would be grave difficulties.
Not just that I was actively opposed
And so was every other man, woman and child
On that there train.
I was afraid they would kill me.
I may look stupid but I'm not
So simple as to think your name
Is Elizabeth Brown. Well. All right
My name is Veronica Forrest-Thomson.

Agamemnon was King of the Achaians at the time,
Priam, of the Trojans, Theseus, of the Athenians.
And like all Good Kings, they are dead.
In my day it was the done thing to side
With the Trojans for no better reason
Than that they lost. But me I back
Winners every time.
Mary Shelley may go to hell
As she thought she was going to anyway
And take Frankinsense with her.
I want her husband, alive and well.
Who, of course, also got killed.
Hardly surprising if he made a habit
Of reading Aiscylos while sailing.
He wasn't reading Aiscylos when he drowned.
Got cremated like a pagan king.
Not Agamemnon who, as I said, was king at the time
And lost, murderer of his daughter
Killed by his wife and (other) daughter.
Killed by his death killing his life.
Stabbed in the back in his bath.
I think of it every time I have a bath.
Though I have no sympathy at all
For that daughter and son.
I think it is unfair that Helen
Had everything, immortal beauty,
Lovers, cities destroyed and battles
Fought about her. And she just came home
And calmly went around being Menelaus' wife
While her twin sister, Clytemnestra
Was murdered by her son and daughter.
And the Athenians acquitted them.
They would do, a nation of sophists.
Always betraying their allies and torturing
Women and children and enslaving people.
They even killed Socrates, their one good man,
Then Plato tried to be a philosopher king.
And got enslaved for his pains.

I wish they had kept him enslaved.
He escaped, of course, and wrote books
About how he would do it better
If he was in charge. All poets do that.
They are just as incompetent as the rest
If they try to organise things.
As witness my own efforts in that direction
Or those of my avatar, Agamemnon,
Who, as I say came home and was killed in his bath
Killing his wife and his daughter.
And if you don't know about this you ought to.
Read it in the *Iliad,* read it in the *Odyssey,*
Do not read it in Freud who is always wrong
Although even Freud didn't deserve a son like Lacan.
But first and last read me, the beloved
Who was killed in the general slaughter.
But rise again like John Donne
(read him too) I, Helen, I Iseult, I Guenevere,
I Clytemnestra and many more to come.
I did it, I myself, killing the King my father
Killing the King my mother, joining the King my brother.
It is the kick, my love, and not the nightingale
I like larking up kicks myself
But not kicking.
They that have power to hurt and do so
Should not be blamed by Shakespeare or anyone else
For hurting though such is the race of poets
That they will blame them anyway.
However it is a pretty productive process
Especially if one may be plumber as well as poet
And thus unstop the drain as well as writing
Poetic Artifice "Pain stopped play" and
Several other books and poems including
1974 and All That (seriously though)
I, Veronica did it, truth-finding, truth-seeking
Muck-raking, bringing victory.
It was a horse, of course, in which the warriors hid
Pretending to bring peace

And they wouldn't speak to me, crouching in the dark
Like a lot of fools, hearing the voice of the goddess
In an alien city, I speak your tongue in my own city:
Cambridge or Camelot and you won't listen to me
Advised, of course, by Odyssos, solicitor, betrayer.
And when they had killed all the men, raped all the women etc.
Agamemnon came home and, as I said, was stabbed by his wife
In his bath. Anyway it is the lark, my love,
And not the nightingale. I follow the sacred footsteps of
Hippolyta, the blest, the best
That has been said or spoken well in any tongue
Read John Donne—the memorable dun.
Don't read Matthew Arnold; he's a fool
I am not Prince Thomas Aquinas F.H. Eliot
I am not an attendant lord either.
I am the king who lives.
Spring surprised us, running through the market square
And we stopped in Prynne's rooms in a shower of pain
And went on in sunlight into the University Library
And ate yogurt and talked for an hour.
You, You, grab the reins.
Drink as much as you can and love as much as you can
And work as much as you can
For you can't do anything when you are dead.

The motto of this poem heed
And do you it employ:
Waste not and want not while you're here
The possibles of joy.

RICHARD II

The wiring appears to be five years old
and is in satisfactory condition.
The insulation resistance is zero.
This reading would be accounted for by the very damp condition of
    the building.
If you come up the stairs on the left side you will see
A band of dense cumulus massed on the banister.
Whatever you do, do not touch the clouds.
Forever again before after and always

In the light of the quiet night and the dark of the quiet noon
I awoke by a day side and I walked in time's room.
To the end of the long wall and the back of the straight floor
I stepped with my years' clutch and the dark of my days' doom.

For the sight of the deep sad and the swell of the short bright
Bid me flee waste of the time web and the long hand
On a life's weft and the grey warp in the year's cloak
For a long shade laps a short stand.

The terms left right front and rear are used
as if one is standing outside the building
facing the front elevation.
Specialists are carrying mirrors to the bedroom.
They are stacked beneath the window three foot deep.
Whatever you do, do not look in the mirror.
Again before forever after and always

The step to and the step back from the still glass in the long wall
Flung the glance wide from the old field and the brown scene.
And the glance broke at the pale horse on the glass turf
While the door swung where the window should have been.

With the ghosts gone and the wall flat as the clock's tick
With a blood stopped and a bone still I squeezed glue from my cold
    glove

And I turned back to my smashed self and the few looks pierced my
    own doll
From the back-lash of the time brick and the last wall of an old love.

In the joinery timbers there is new infestation
And a damp-proof course is urgently needed.
Say a few prayers to the copper wire.
Technicians are placing flowers in the guttering
They are welding the roof to a patch of sky
Whatever you do, do not climb on the roof.
Before forever after again and always.

limpid eyelid

S/Z

J'étais plongé dans une de ces
rêveries profondes
qui saissit tout le monde
même un homme frivole
au sein des fêtes les plus tumultueuses.

Au fêtes tumultueuses:
rêveries profondes.

I was sunk in one of those
profound daydreams
which grab everyone
even a trivial man
in the middle of the most violent parties.

At violent parties:
profound daydreams.

That is one of the rules Balzac uses
and Barthes notices.
There are many other rules,
but I don't want to mention them.
We can—some of us—sometimes
forget the whole problem.
I mean the only problem:
What is true.
I write no question mark
after that question.

There are a few answers, such as:
Literature matters.
What else is there.
What am I going to do with my life.
Write another book, I suppose.
What else is there.
I expect no answer.

Poems teach one that much:
to expect no answer.
But keep on asking questions;
that is important.
Just hope the house doesn't fall down
for I have no insurance.

Je suis plongée dans une de ces
rêveries profondes
qui saissit tout le monde
même une femme frivole
au sein des fêtes tumultueuses.

LEMON AND ROSEMARY
for Catherine Cullen

Nobody. I, myself.
Shooting live subjects in pictures sung with imagination and wrung
    with truth.
Dean knew it was blackmail.

Though my deserted frying pans lie around me
I do not want to make it cohere.
Hung up to dry for fishing lines on the side of grey wharf of Lethe.
Old, we love each other and know more.

Is this a chisel that I see before me.
If so I want to hack my name on the bedroom door.

A star shines on the hour of our meeting:
Lucifer, son of morning. And
Thanks for your lighter I have forgotten the matches.

O, why do I hate doctors so?
There was a time some years ago . . .
But do dial one o o o o

On the best battle fields
No dead bodies

Appendices

1: AN IMPERSONAL STATEMENT

[In Veronica Forrest and Cavan McCarthy, *Veronicavan: Program of a Reading at the Bristol Arts Centre, 30 December 1967.*]

Veronica Forrest was born in Malaya in 1947, but educated in Scotland with an early specialisation in Greek and Latin which has infected her with a, perhaps exaggerated, respect for impersonality and formal values in art. It was this which first aroused her interest in concrete poetry as an antidote to the formlessness and academicism of the Movement writers and the introversion of the so-called "confessional" poets. It was also seemingly the first real re-exploration of language-form since the Eliot–Pound revolution and its American offshoots and as such most suited to the expression of a contemporary environment. This went along with a consuming passion for science, especially in exploring the possibilities of expressing the new universe of nuclear and astro-physics and in trying to treat human situations in terms of such patterns. In practice however she has found the semantic element almost impossible to exclude and now regards concrete more as a means than as an end in itself. There has been a similar modification of her previous partisanship of impersonality with the realisation that what makes any work of art valuable is its dynamic expression of the inter-relation between subject/object which is often expressed in the content/form tension, and that it is impossible entirely to exclude the individual "vision" though this in the interests of presenting a balanced re-creation of reality should be kept to the minimum. If there must be a justification for making poems it is surely that they provide the same kind of data concerning the inter-actions of man and his environmental situations as does science only in different terms in the man-impregnation medium of language, in fact, and by extending the exploration of language-possibilities extend man's capacity to articulate and experience while at the same time providing, one hopes, new and pleasurable objects for experience in the form' of "works of art". On a more personal level, by showing what can be done with an experience or subject to, perhaps, help others to live their own experiences more fully and richly.

2: CONTRIBUTOR'S NOTE

[In *Solstice*, no. 9 (Cambridge, 1969), to which the author contributed the following four poems: 'Fêtes Nationales & Zazie in the London Underground', 'The Blue Book', 'Letters of Ezra Pound', and 'Epitaph for an Un-Named Priestess'. This note was developed as the 'Note' to *Language-Games* (1971). The four poems were not included in that volume.]

The poems attempt to set up a tension between the meaning of the statements which they steal from other contexts such as Pound's letters, the later work of Wittgenstein, and conversations, and the structure of the poem itself. They share the theme of the impossibility of expressing, or even of experiencing, a non-linguistic reality. The process is a reflection of our constant attempt to integrate disparate levels of knowledge, such for instance of the experience of being in a particular place, Cambridge, or encountering particular ideas—Wittgenstein comes in again here as his notion of language games suggests that basically what we do with our words is what we do with our experience of living.

3: NOTE

[Printed following the poems in *Language-Games* (Leeds, New Poets Award 2. School of English Press. University of Leeds. 1971).]

Most of these poems are obviously about the experience of being engaged in a certain activity, in a certain place, at a certain time: the activity, research in English Literature, the place, Cambridge, the time, 1968-69. The attempt has been to deal with these elements as part of a "historical present" in which past language-forms, whether borrowed from poetry, letters, speech, or the dictionary, are made into a framework for a present act of articulation. This act looks for a form to express the poems' underlying theme: the impossibility of expressing some non-linguistic reality, or even of experiencing such a reality. Wittgenstein comes in here as I take his work to be the most stimulating exposition of the complexities involved in this view; but his ideas are also used to explore the second main pre-occupation of the poems, the relationship between "pure" intellectual activity, in fields such as philosophy and theoretical science, and their appearance in an "applied" context, as one element among others in one's attempt to make sense of concrete experience.

It seems to me that this interaction is best seen as a juxtaposition of varying ways of using language for one is thus able completely to absorb the non-linguistic constituents of the experience into the art of language; questions of knowledge become questions of technique. This results in the setting up of a tension between the meaning of the ideas and statements in their original context and their appearance in the poem; they are in a sense different expressions, not because they refer to another area of experience—it is their own original area of reference that I have wished to make part of the subject-matter of poetry—but because they are used in a different way.

This kind of tension can be seen as a special case of the conflicts that arise from our constant attempt to integrate disparate levels of knowledge; it thus ties in with the exploration of the present sense of the past through its language-forms. At the vaguest level it could be subsumed under the grandiose heading of "Art versus Life"; for basically what we do with our words is what we do with our experience of living.

There is the opportunity to turn theoretical debate and abstract statement into a means of technical experiment in the actual medium of poetry, to explore new formal possibilities while extending the range of material dealt with. This involves an assimilation, not merely of the ideas but of the speech-forms of the relevant areas of discourse and even their methods of typographical layout. Certain poems here tentatively explore such possibilities. It will be seen that this leads to a new stress on the importance of "subject" in a poem; but because it is not the ideas merely but the actual linguistic forms that are to be the object of attention, the new kind of subject will be one that can be approached and even defined in terms of formal experimentation. The process is one of smashing and rebuilding the forms of thought. Thus one might be permitted to feel a certain affinity with those who see the role of the University as a subversion of accepted social reality. The means may be destructive however, but the end, or rather each particular end—for there are as many ends as there are poems—is not. The construction of poems becomes the record of a series of individual thresholds of the experience of being conscious; they form the definition, or affirmation, in time and in language, of human identity.

4: PREFACE

[In *On the Periphery* (Cambridge, Street Editions. 1976).]

The mysteries of this book are partially summed up in its title. After the head-on collision with non-poetic languages in my previous work I was faced by a stylistic situation on the periphery of traditional poetry. The sequence of pieces here represents—apart from their individual merit—a series of strategies for dealing with this difficulty. A difficulty which must confront any poet at this time who can take and make the art a new and serious opponent—perhaps even a successful alternative—to the awfulness of the modern world. I have argued elsewhere that this awfulness cannot be overcome with entire reference to the non-verbal world for the non-verbal world, like other deities, helps only those who help themselves. And what poetry gains from that world is gained through language, through the very languages that give us the world. For poetry, as always, has special access to aspects of language distinct from the aspect of communication. These simple, and very complex, mechanisms have been largely lost in English poetry since the 'twenties. So that my concern with French poetry and poetic theory and with ideas associated with "Structuralism" is a manœuvre of style, of verbal detail, as well as a manœuvre of theme and of social significance.

Hence the graph of this book begins in the extreme of aleatory poems, moves into simple lyricism confronting the claims of the external world with stylistic simplicity, reaches, in "The Dying Gladiator", an extreme of both technical and thematic complexity, and ends, in "The Lady of Shalott", by recapturing the right to speak directly through the traditional ranges of rhymed stanza.

The turning point comes in "Pastoral" where I realise in practice what I have long known in theory: that it is precisely those non-meaningful aspects of language—rhyme, rhythm and stanzaic metre are only the most obvious—which are poetry's strength and its defence. What had been tendentious obscurity of meaning becomes, therefore, a tendentious refusal of meaning, except the minimum needed to create verbal form at all, this coupled with a more assured and more traditional formal experimentation in the two Odes, the epitaph on Ezra Pound, the assertion of affinity with the past of English poetry, especially the neglected past of the late nineteenth-century, in "Strike".

Thus "The Lady of Shalott" is both the end of this quest for a lost imaginative freedom made actual in verbal detail and a beginning which, freed from sterile self-absorption, will move on to create new artifices of eternity. Thus also, the last poem "Sonnet" is the love poem I have tried throughout to write straight and have been held back from by these technical and sociological difficulties. For, as to theme, this book is the chart of three quests. The quest for a style already discussed, the quest for a subject other than the difficulty of writing, and the quest for another human being. Indeed such equation of love with knowledge and the idea of style as their reconciliation is as old as the art itself, for the other person is the personification of the other, the unknown, the external world and all one's craft is necessary to catch him. And, of course, being caught as a poetic fiction, as a real person he is gone.

And so one is left with the poems—what they do and what they suggest as possible. "For us there is only the trying / The rest is not our business".

5: RICHARD II

[Written to introduce Veronica Forrest-Thomson's commissioned poem 'Richard II' at the public reading in Southwark Cathedral of *Poems for Shakespeare* (part of the Shakespeare birthday celebrations) on 26 April 1975. A memoir of the circumstances of the reading, in her absence, of the poem and her chosen passage from Shakespeare, *Richard II*, V, v, 42–66, was published in A. Rudolf, ed., *Poems for Shakespeare*, 4 (London, Globe Playhouse Publications. 1976).]

This poem requires a little introduction which I hope will help you to understand what I am trying to do. I picked the play, *Richard II*, because it is one of my favourites and because it is one of Shakespeare's most striking uses of the image of the actor as hero. This image, of course, accompanies far-reaching meditation on the relationship between appearance and reality. The difference between appearance and reality and how poetry may bridge this difference by creating imaginative orders of words—for it is language that really mediates between the world of appearances and internal reality or the world of reality and internal appearances depending on one's philosophical position—has long fascinated me both in theory and practice. This problem and the problem of time are closely connected, for it is through time that appearance and reality interact, through time that poetry moves, and *Richard II* is therefore a play much concerned with time. These are the themes then about which or around which I wished to construct my poem but it would not do to sit down and write a versified meditation on time change appearance and reality. For this there are several reasons. First—though perhaps I should not let this out—I don't have very many or very new ideas about these topics at least just now. Second, ideas are not simply assimilated into poems direct but must make their way through the organisation of technical devices ranging from metaphor to metre. Third, and most important, I believe that at the present time poetry must progress by deliberately trying to defeat the expectations of its readers or hearers, especially the expectation that they will be able to extract meaning from a poem. A poem must work to transform the area of linguistic meaning into a technical device like rhythm or metre. Consequently the poem in question sets out to look as if it were a meditation on time appearance and reality while in fact using these themes as points in its organisation as a metrical formal structure. It includes the normal expectations of the reader/listener but seeks to upset these in the interests of stressing the importance of non-meaningful levels of language in poetry. This is a more difficult undertaking from writing an ordinary poem as the balance of meaning and non-meaning must be very precariously set up. I think it must be attempted, however, if poetry is once again to take its place as an experimental exploration of the human mind working in language.

BIBLIOGRAPHY AND RECORDINGS

A: DISSERTATION & PUBLISHED LITERARY CRITICISM BY THE AUTHOR

'Poetry as Knowledge: The Use of Science by Twentieth-Century Poets', Ph.D dissertation (Cambridge University, 1971).

'Irrationality and Artifice: A Problem in Recent Poetics', *The British Journal of Aesthetics*, vol. II, no. 2 (Spring 1971), pp. 123–133.

'Levels in Poetic Convention', *Journal of European Studies*, vol. 2 (1972), pp. 35–51.

'The Ritual of Reading *Salammbô*', *Modern Language Review*, vol. 67, no. 4 (Spring 1972), pp. 787–798.

'Au-delà du réel: La Poésie anglaise moderne à l'heure du choix', *Chroniques de l'art vivant*, no. 29 (Paris, avril 1972), pp. 24–25. Translation by Michel Canavaggio of 'Beyond Reality . . .'

'Beyond Reality: Orders of Possibility in Modern English Poetry', *Fuse*, no. 1 ([Cambridge], June 1972), pp. 20–23.

'Necessary Artifice: Form and Theory in the Poetry of *Tel Quel*', *Language and Style*, vol. 7, no. 1 (Winter 1973), pp. 3–26.

'Rational Artifice: Some Remarks on the Poetry of William Empson', *Yearbook of English Studies*, vol. 4 (Winter 1974), pp. 225–238.

'Dada, Unrealism and Contemporary Poetry', *Twentieth-Century Studies*, vol. 12 (December 1974), pp. 77–93.

'Unrealism as the Poetic Mode for this Century', *Spindrift*, no. 1 (Canterbury, [1977?]), pp. 16–27.

Poetic Artifice: A Theory of Twentieth-Century Poetry (Manchester, Manchester University Press, and New York, St. Martin's Press, 1978).

'La Planète séparée: John Donne et William Empson', *Cahiers de l'Herne, Les Dossiers H: John Donne*, ed., J.-M. Benoist (Paris, L'Age d'homme, 1983), pp. 213–246.

B: PUBLISHED LETTERS FROM THE AUTHOR

'Extract from a Letter to the Editor', [dated 7/5/72], *Landseer*, vol. 1, no. 3 ([Cambridge], October 1972).

'A Letter to G .S. Fraser', dated 19/8/74, *Adam International Review*, vol. xxxix, nos. 391-393 (London, 1975).

C: PERSONAL TRIBUTES TO THE AUTHOR

Isobel Armstrong, 'Feeling and Playing', *Adam* ... , id.

Charles Bernstein, "Artifice of Absorption", *Paper Air*, vol. 4, no. 1 (Philadelphia, Singing Horse Press, 1987), makes substantial reference to Forrest-Thomson's writings.

Andrew Crozier, 'Dodo You're Not Dead', *Printed Circuit* (Cambridge, Street Editions, 1974); repr. *All Where Each Is* (London & Berkeley, Allardyce, Barnett, 1985), makes substantial reference to Forrest-Thomson's writings.

G.S. Fraser, 'Veronica: A Tribute', id.

Graham Hough, 'Foreword', *Poetic Artifice: A Theory of Twentieth Century Poetry* (Manchester, Manchester University Press, and New York, St. Martin's Press, 1978).

F.Q. Lawson, 'The Outrageous Friend', *Adam* . . . , id.

[Tim Longville, ed.] , *For Rolf Dieter Brinkmann and Veronica Forrest-Thomson*, a memorial anthology of poems and a translation by Anthony Barnett, Michael Chamberlain, Andrew Crozier, Denis Goacher, John Hall, Kris Hemensley, John James, Tim Longville, Douglas Oliver, John Riley (Pensnett, Staffs., Ferry, Great Works, Grosseteste, 1975).

Edwin Morgan, 'Unfinished Poems: A Sequence for Veronica Forrest-Thomson', *Poems of Thirty Years* (Manchester, Carcanet, 1982).

J.H. Prynne, 'Veronica Forrest-Thomson: A Personal Memoir', *On the Periphery* (Cambridge, Street Editions, 1976).

Anthony Rudolf, 'Introduction' and 'Postscript: Veronica Forrest-Thomson', *Poems for Shakespeare, 4* (London, Globe Playhouse Publications, 1976) [see Appendix 5].

Robert Sheppard, 'Parody and Pastoral: A Text or Commentary for Veronica Forrest-Thomson', *Hymns to the Gods in Which My Typewriter Believes* (Exeter, Stride Publications, 2006).

D: SOUND RECORDINGS OF THE AUTHOR

Essex Arts Festival, University of Essex, 27 April, 1967. Deposited in the British Library, National Sound Archive, ref. T7209. The author reads the following poems: 'Through the Looking Glass', 'According to the Script', 'Clown (by Paul Klee)', section I of 'Subatomic Symphony'.

Anthony Rudolf's London apartment, 14 June, 1973. Private recording and unpublished transcript. Informal discussion on poetry with David Beugger, Richard Burns, Veronica Forrest-Thomson, William Oxley, Lawrence Pitt-Kethley, Anthony Rudolf, Geoffrey Squires, John Welch, Augustus Young.

Cambridge Poetry Festival, 17 April, 1975. Deposited in the British Library, National Sound Archive, ref. T6013. The author reads the following poems: 'The Garden of Proserpine', 'Cordelia: or, "A Poem Should not Mean, but Be"', 'S/Z', 'Lemon and Rosemary', 'The Lady of Shalott', 'Strike'.

Cambridge Poetry Festival, 18 April, 1975. Deposited in the British Library, National Sound Archive, ref. T6023. Poetry Forum: 'Unrealism and Death in Contemporary Poetry' with Michel Couturier and Veronica Forrest-Thomson; introduced by Richard Burns. [Denis Roche was scheduled but did not appear.]

NOTES

ABBREVIATIONS USED IN THE NOTES

C   *Cordelia: or, 'A Poem Should not Mean, but Be'* ([Leicester], Omens Poetry Pamphlet, no. 2, 1974); [i] denotes the first unnumbered section; ii denotes the second numbered section.

CPF   A tape recording of the author reading her poems at the Cambridge Poetry Festival, 17 April 1975; deposited in the British Library, National Sound Archive.

ES   *Earth Ship*, no. 12, 'A Womens Issue' [*sic*] (Southampton, October 1972).

L-G   *Language-Games* (Leeds, New Poets Award 2, School of English Press, University of Leeds, 1971).

'LP'   Section of *OP* entitled 'Last Poems'.

O   *Omens*, vol. 3, no. 2 (Leicester, January 1974); contains the five poems in Cii.

OA   A copy of *O* with amendments and comments in the author's hand dated 12/1/74.

OED   *Oxford English Dictionary*.

OP   *On the Periphery* (Cambridge, Street Editions, 1976).

'OP'   Typescripts of *OP*; 73 denotes a copy known in November 1973 and used for the present volume; 75 denotes a copy known in May 1975 and used for *OP*.

'P'   Notebook entitled 'Pomes' containing drafts of many of the poems in *OP*, as well as other poems.

PA   *Poetic Artifice: A Theory of Twentieth-Century Poetry* (Manchester, Manchester University Press, and New York, St. Martin's Press, 1978).

TAQ   *Twelve Academic Questions* (Cambridge, The Author, February 1970).

UCL   Manuscripts and typescripts in the *Tlaloc* Archive deposited in The Library, University College London.

UNCOLLECTED EARLY POEMS

Poems known only in manuscript or typescript are apparently previously unpublished.

'The Room'
Equator, [no. 2] ([Liverpool, 1966]

'Sagittarius'
Manuscript dated 28/11/66, the author's nineteenth birthday.

'Still A-Building'
Breakthru, vol. 6, no. 32 (Haywards Heath, Sussex, January–February 1967).

'The White Magician'
Continuum, no. 5 (Bailrigg, Lancs, [1967])

'Literary Historian'
Continuum . . .

'Social Contract'
Phoenix, New Quarterly Series, no. 2 (Belfast, Summer 1967).

'The Needle's'
Equator, no. 5 (Liverpool 1967).

'Beginners Please'
Equator, no. 6 (Liverpool 1967).

'Epicurus'
Typescript; the author's Liverpool address on the verso of the last page.

'Don't Bite the Hand that Throws Dust in Your Eyes'
Typescript. Printed in Veronica Forrest and Cavan McCarthy, *Veronicavan: Program of a Reading at the Bristol Arts Centre, 30 December 1967*.

'Grapes for Grasshoppers'
Veronicavan . . .

'Computer 97/100DV'
Veronicavan . . . Also with very different lineation in *Continuum* . . .

'Habitat'
Manuscript; typescript in UCL. Printed in *Tlaloc*, no. 15 (Blackburn, 1967).

'fine'
Manuscript in UCL.

'Landscape with Yellow Birds'
Typescript in UCL.

'Atomic Disintegration'
Part manuscript part typescript in UCL.

'At Work: / At Play:'
Typescript in UCL.

'2 Staircase Poems'
Typescript in UCL.

'Catalog'
text, no. 2 / no. 1 new series (Arnold, Notts., Autumn 1968).

'Language Lesson for a Schizophrenic Age'
text . . .

'Tooth'
Manuscript dated 17/5/68.

'1, 28'
Poetry Review, vol. LX, no. 1 (London, Spring 1969).

'Fêtes Nationales & Zazie in the London Underground'
Solstice, no. 9 (Cambridge, 1969).

'The Blue Book'
Solstice, no. 9 (Cambridge, 1969).

'Letters of Ezra Pound'
Solstice, no. 9 (Cambridge, 1969).

'Epitaph for an Un-Named Priestess'
Typescript. Printed in *Solstice*, no. 9 (Cambridge, 1969).

'Individuals'
Typescript; the author's Cambridge address on the verso of the last page.

'Variations from Sappho'
The first poem printed in *TAQ* and the only poem in that volume not reprinted in *L-G*.

LANGUAGE-GAMES

The first thirteen poems were reprinted, with no important differences, from *Twelve Academic Questions* (1970), a pamphlet typed and published by the author. The first poem in *TAQ*, 'Variations from Sappho', was not reprinted in *L-G* and is included here in 'Uncollected Early Poems'. The 'Note' to *L-G* is printed in Appendix 3.

ON THE PERIPHERY

On the Periphery (1976) was prepared posthumously from a photocopied typescript provided by Jonathan Culler in May 1975. In addition to the author's collection of that title, *OP* attempted to gather further poems under the title 'Last Poems'. In preparing the present edition, 'OP' 75 was compared with a photocopied typescript received by J.H. Prynne from the author in November 1973. Reference was also made to the pamphlet *Cordelia: or, 'A Poem Should not Mean, but Be'* (1974) which contains a number of the poems in *OP*. The text used here is 'OP' 73. This typescript consists of a contents page, a preface, and the poems. The last two poems, 'Canzon' and 'In Memoriam', do not appear on the contents page. Two poems. 'To R.Z. and M.W.' and 'On Reading Mr. Melville's *Tales*', are added in the author's hand to the contents page in their respective positions. Some of the poems are typed by the author; others are typed on another typewriter possibly by a professional typist. All but the title poem of the ten poems in *C* are included in 'OP' 73. All ten were reprinted, some in substantially different versions, in *OP*; but two poems. 'Sonnet' and 'The Garden of Proserpine', were erroneously included in 'LP'. 'OP' 75 partly pre-dates 'OP' 73: some leaves do not include amendments in the author's hand on the same originals used for both photocopies; five poems in 'OP' 75 are not in typescript at all but in photocopies of the pages of C[1]. The ordering of OP, including its division into two sections, the title section and 'LP', is not in accord with the 'Preface' which identifies 'Sonnet' as the last poem of the title collection. There is no evidence for the ordering and division in OP, and there is other contradictory evidence: of the eight poems printed in 'LP' two, 'Sonnet' and 'The Garden of Proserpine', are included in 'OP' 73; and two, 'In Memoriam' and 'Canzon', are included among the poems in 'OP' 73, although not listed on the contents page. Two further poems, 'Since the Siege and Assault Was Ceased in Troy . . .' and 'Cordelia . . .', although not included in 'OP' 73 nevertheless appear in draft manuscripts, in a notebook entitled 'Pomes', together with other poems belonging to the title collection, dating their gestation, at least, from the same period. It does not seem possible to establish with certainty either the author's latest intentions for the ordering and contents of the title collection or, in some cases, which of several variants should take precedence over others. For example, C post-dates 'OP' 73 yet includes variants printed in journals predating 'OP' 73. In following here the contents page of 'OP' 73, the position of 'Sonnet' is now in accord with the 'Preface'; other poems, including those possibly intended for the collection but not listed on the contents page, are included here in 'Further Poems'. The 'Preface' to OP is printed in Appendix 4. The ordering of the poems in C is as follows:

[I]	II
Sonnet	An Arbitrary Leaf
The Garden of Proserpine	Pastoral
In Memoriam	The Ear of Dionysios
Canzon	Ode: The Lady of Shalott
Cordelia	Strike

'On Naming of Shadows'
In the typescript the third stanza has been compressed, almost certainly in error, into seven lines. The lineation restored here follows an earlier version printed, with minor differences, in Landseer, vol. 1, no. 3 ([Cambridge], October 1972); and ES.

'An Arbitrary Leaf'
An earlier version was printed in O, and C. OA adds 'for Roland Barthes':

Printed in natural colours we find a way always
to deny the world; even its "aerial view" from
"the tower itself". A biro-cross marks the place
where our arcades and buttresses dissolved in air;
but still it is a "carte-postale de luxe"
reminder of "an extraordinary experience".
These occasions have a way of multiplying:

the treads are uneven with "five-hundred-years of wear"
and darken to a height of—wouldn't you say?—
about the same number of feet. This would never
be allowed in England, such sudden and insouciant
lack of the next step. Give me your hand.

Shall we exorcise these colours that contrast us
with our evening walk consciously encoded
in the voice and gesture of our shadowy design
to undermine the objects on its path.

And so this ivy leaf, in lack of colour
in perfected shape may be "like" fan-vaulting
(communication having been accepted) but no
finality in such a text can justify a reference
to Maillezais, or Clément and his castle, Villandraut.

'Drinks with a Mythologue'
An earlier version entitled 'Drinks with a Metalogue', with otherwise
minor differences, was printed in *A Range of Curtains* (Hebden Bridge,
1973) with the note 'see Roland Barthes'.

'Address to the Reader, from Pevensey Sluice'
An earlier version, with very different lineation, was printed in *ES*; a
draft manuscript on two leaves torn from a notebook (not 'P') is dated
20/8/71:

If it were quicksand you could sink; something needing a light touch
soon and so simply takes its revenge. Slightly
west of Goodwin Sands the land hardens again with history, resists
the symbol. Chalk requires an allegorical hand,
or employee of Sussex Water Board to set a notice here:
DANGER SUBMERGED STRUCTURES

and all at once Transformational Grammar "peoples" the
    "emotional landscape"
with refutation. You may hear its melancholy
long withdrawing roar even on Dover beach watching the undertow
of all those trips across to France.

Follow the reader and his writer, those emblematic persons along
    their mythic route
charting its uncertain curves and camber;
for to be true to any other you must—and I shall never now—
    recover
a popular manœuvre known mostly as, turn over
and go to sleep.

'On the Periphery'
An earlier version, with very different lineation, was printed in *ES:*

Ducks flee into the undergrowth like eponymous heroes
as we approach the past, walking slowly on a path
beside a waterway or something liquid.

These stories are committed to writing
only when they have reached (we have reached)
a high degree of sophistication. Sanctioned &
solacing polythene buttercups strew the way
with images of inevitable "natural" regeneration.

Somewhere the table's set far from the traffic jam,
thus she spoke, turning, mov'd the third heaven,
that popular memory. So many recipes now set revolving
&, Oh, that reminds me (poetry functions as tribal mnemonic)
who are we having for dinner tomorrow?

'Approaching the Library'
l.13: the typescript reads 'Devil's Dike' but this is not usual orthography.

'Facsimile of a Waste Land'
'OP' 73 has an amendment in the author's hand from '. . . the Waste
Land', absent from 'OP' 75.

'Pastoral'
Printed as a poster in collaboration with the artist Anne Zefferelli; one in a series of poster poems published by the Cambridge Poetry Festival 1975. The text is in the author's hand; l.13 reads 'Like, our . . .' An earlier version was printed in *Fuse*, no. 2 (Cambridge, November 1972); and, with minor differences, in *O, C.,* and *PA (PA* l.12 reads '. . . a car's . . .*):
OA adds 'for J.H.Prynne / il miglior fabbro'; and below the poem:

> my first head-on collision successfully
> averted
>   the other   the
>   ↓ two   ↑ ↓ other
>   ↑ seconds me
> long vehicle | _{me}
>
> They are our creatures clover, and they love us
> through the long summer meadows' diesel fumes.
> Smooth as their scent and contours clear however
> less than enough to compensate for names.
>
> Jagged are names and not our creatures
> neither in sense or fullness like the flowers.
> Raised voices in a car or by a river
> remind us of the world that is not ours.
>
> Silence in grass and solace in blank verdure
> summon the frightful glare of nouns and nerves.
> The gentle foal linguistically wounded
> squeals like the car's brakes, like our twisted words.

'Le Signe (Cygne)'
A draft manuscript in 'P' and a draft typescript are entitled 'For the Third Time Shake the Snow off Your Boots'; a draft manuscript on a leaf torn from a notebook (not 'P') entitled 'Le Cygne (Signe)' is dated 1/3/72.

'The Ear of Dionysios: Ode'
O and *C* print the title without 'Ode'; 'Ode' is added in the author's hand to 'OP'.
ll.15–24 comprise two prose paragraphs; there is no evidence whether

or not the author intended right margin justification.

l.22: the author's orthography is 'paidophilia' (in *OED*), not as printed in *OP.*

O and *C* print the inset lines (26, 28, 30, etc.) with a common left margin.

OA has three amendments: one appears in the author's hand in the typescript (l.36 originally reading 'but refill the flask in island lochs'); but two do not:

l.30: 'You can't get back on the other shore'.

l.45: 'my steering veers',

'Le Pont traversé: Ode'

ll.9–40 comprise five prose paragraphs; there is no evidence whether or not the author intended right margin justification.

'Strike'

First printed, with minor differences, in *O* and *C*.

CPF has the following differences:

l.7 repeats 'that lover' five times.

l.29 gives '. . . a quest.' (as do *O* and *C*).

l.30 gives ' . . .-before feel about it.' (as do *O* and *C*).

'The Lady of Shalott: Ode'

First printed, with minor differences, entitled 'Ode: The Lady of Shalott' in *O* and *C*; and entitled 'The Lady of Shalott' in *PA*.

l.3: *PA* prints 'For if what we seek cannot be truth,'.

l.10: the typescript reads 'No one would wish . . .'; *O, C, PA*, and CPF give 'No one would care . . .' and, exceptionally, this has been accepted.

l.21: *OA* adds a period also printed in *PA*.

l.27: the author's orthography in 'OP', *O* and *C* is 'Leucritius'; *OA* deletes the 'e'.

'The Garden of Proserpine'

There is no dedication in the typescript. *C*, from where this poem was taken for 'LP' (there is no typescript in 'OP'75), prints 'in memoriam A.C. Swinburne'. CPF has' . . . which is of course the title of a poem by Swinburne but I've taken it over. It's for Catherine Cullen.'

l.69: CPF omits '. . . as those who refuse to try.'

l.73: CPF has 'And we still loved . . .'

FURTHER POEMS

This section contains six of the eight poems included in 'LP'; and three uncollected poems, two of which were apparently previously unpublished before their appearance in *Collected Poems and Translations* (1990).

'A Plea for Excuses'
Unpublished typescript. Draft manuscripts on the first pages of 'P' date the poem from the same period as 'OP'. The following lines are added to the typescript in the author's hand to the right of ll.3–5: 'These thoughts are / not of us but of our / creatures. It is the indirect / free style'; possibly an alternative.
l.25: the typescript and a draft manuscript read 'Then . . .' but the sense, confirmed by several trial amendments in an earlier draft, requires 'There . . .'

'Since the Siege and Assault Was Ceased in Troy . . .'
Typescript in 'OP' 75. Printed in 'LP'. Draft manuscript in 'P', headed 'Project for "Gawain and the Green Knight"', with the section titles 'The Beheading Game', 'The Temptation', 'The Exchange of Winnings', dates the poem from the same period as 'OP'.

'I have a little hour-glass' and *'I have a little nut-tree'*
Unpublished. Draft manuscript in 'P' dates the poems from the same period as *OP* [see also 'Facsimile of a Waste Land']; manuscript (including drafts) on both sides of a leaf torn from a notebook (not 'P'); the drafts are followed by 'This poem has now been metamorphosed— the nursery rhyme meant to give frivolity and (I hope) a sort of childish menace to the cliché material—into:'

I have a little hour-glass'
. . .
'and finally, unrecognisably:'

I have a little nut-tree
. . .

'In Memoriam'
Typescript in 'OP' 73 (but not listed in the contents) entitled 'In Memoriam J.D.C.' Printed in *C*, entitled 'In Memoriam', from where the poem was taken for 'LP' (there is no typescript in 'OP' 75).

'Canzon'
Typescript in 'OP' 73 (but not listed in the contents). Printed in C from where the poem was taken for 'LP' (there is no typescript in 'OP' 75). l.40: C and 'LP' print 'And yet I would not love' in error; the typescript reads: 'And yet I would not not love' as the sense requires.

'Cordelia: or, "A Poem Should not Mean, but Be"'
Printed in C from where the poem was taken for 'LP'. Only a draft typescript, entitled 'Pain Stopped Play or "The Twilight of the Gods" / for the Star', has been found. A draft manuscript, entitled 'Tradition and the Individual Talent', on the last pages of 'P' dates the gestation of the poem from the same period as 'OP'.
CPF has the following differences:
l.66: 'In fact I never . . .'
l.78: 'Riddle me riddle me randy ree'.
ll.95–97: omitted.
l.112: '. . . they are all dead.'
l. 153: 'When they try . . .'
l.159: 'It is in the *Iliad,* read it . . .'
ll.170–171: omitted.
l.172: 'They that have . . .'; C and 'LP' print 'They have . . .' in error.
l.181: *'The Profession of Lies'* in place of *'1974 and All That'*.
l.197: omits '—the memorable dun',
l.203: '. . . in a shower of rain'.

'Richard II'
Two typescripts: the first, in 'OP' 75, printed in 'LP'; the second printed in *Poems for Shakespeare,* 4 (London, Globe Playhouse Publications. 1976).
l.28: the typescript used for *Poems for Shakespeare* reads: '. . . the clock tick'; the typescript in 'OP'75 reads: '. . . the clock's tick', which has been accepted.
l.30: both typescripts read '. . . pieced my own doll', almost certainly in error; different errors also occur in both typescripts in 'squeezed' in l.29.
l.39 is added in the author's hand to the first typescript; and typed in the second typescript.
A note intended to accompany the public reading of this commissioned poem is printed in Appendix 5.

'S/Z'
No typescript has been found. Printed, without a title, in *Meantime*, no. 1 (Cambridge, April 1977). CPF gives the title; the author introduces the poem as follows: 'It's called "S/Z" which is the title of a very well known book by Roland Barthes.'

'Lemon and Rosemary'
Typescript in 'OP' 75. Printed in 'LP'. Possibly unfinished; the author reads a variant on CPF and introduces the poem as follows: 'Now this one is really a sort of work in progress. It's not finished and I dare say that I'll alter the word order and line order a bit but I'd like to see how it reads. It's called, with a backwards glance at "garlic and sapphires" [T.S. Eliot, *Four Quartets*, 'Burnt Norton', II, l.1], "Lemon and Rosemary". It's for Catherine Cullen.'
l.15 [CPF l.14]: the author's typewriter does not distinguish 0 from O. Old style numeral [o] is used here in the absence of certainty about the author's intention.

    Though my deserted frying pans lie around me
    I do not want to make it cohere.

    Nobody. I, myself.
    Shooting live subjects in pictures sung with imagination and
        wrung with truth.
    Dean knew it was blackmail.

    Hung up to dry for fishing lines on the side of the grey wharf of
        Lethe.
    Is this a chisel I see before me.
    If so I want to hack my name on the bedroom door.

    A star shines on the hour of our meeting:
    Lucifer, son of the morning. And
    Thanks for your lighter I have forgotten the matches.

    O, why do I hate doctors so?
    There was a time some years ago . . .
    But do dial one o o o o

    On the best battle fields
    No dead bodies

Index of Titles

According to the Script   28
Acrostic   80
Address to the Reader, from Pevensey Sluice   116
A Fortiori   98
Alka-Seltzer Poem   89
Ambassador of Autumn (by Paul Klee)   25
An Arbitrary Leaf   111
Antiphrasis   83
Antiquities   85
A Plea for Excuses   145
Approaching the Library   120
A Reaction to Rings   20
Aries   18
Atomic Disintegration   53
At Work: /At Play: 54
Automat   32

Beginners Please   44

Canzon   150
Catalog   56
Christmas Morning   23
Clown (by Paul Klee)   21
Computer 97/100DV   49
Contours—Homage to Cézanne   27
Conversation on a Benin Head   126
Cordelia: or 'A Poem Should not Mean, but Be'   152
Criteria for Continuing a Series   94

Don't Bite the Hand that Throws Dust in Your Eyes   47
Drinks with a Mythologue   114
Ducks & Rabbits   76

Epicurus   45
Epitaph for a Un-Named Priestess   65

Facsimile of a Waste Land   122
Fêtes Nationales & Zazie in the London Underground   61
fine   51
For the Spider who Frequents Our Bath   109

Gemini   14
Grapes for Grasshoppers   48
Group Theory   57

Habitat   50

Identi-kit   16
Idols of the (Super)Market   81
I have a little hour-glass   148
I have a little nut-tree   148
In Defence of Graham Hough: Style and Stylistics   103
In Defence of Leavis: the Common Pursuit   103
Individuals   67
In Memoriam   149
In Memoriam Ezra Pound   132
In the Greenhouse   17
In This House   22
It Doesn't Matter about Mantrippe   99

January Morning   13

Landscape with Yellow Birds   52
Language Lesson for a Schizophrenic Age   57
Leaving the Library   121
L'Effet du réel   110
Lemon and Rosemary   162
Le Pont traversé: Ode   130
Le Signe (Cygne)   125
Letters of Ezra Pound   64
Literary Historian   41

Michaelmas   73

Notes to Chapter 1,002   95
Not Pastoral Enough   124

1,28   59
On Naming of Shadows   106
On Reading Mr. Melville's *Tales*   119
On the Periphery   117

Pastoral   123

Pfarr-Schmerz (Village-Anguish)   112
Phrase Book   97
Point of View at Noon   19
Provence   24

Richard II   158

Sagittarius   36
Selection Restrictions on Peanuts for Dinner   108
Since the Siege and Assault Was Ceased in Troy . . .   146
Social Contract   42
Sonnet   141
Still A-Building   37
Strike   134
Subatomic Symphony   30
S/Z   160

Taurus   15
The Aquarium   118
The Blue Book   63
The Brown Book   75
The Dying Gladiator   113
The Ear of Dionysios: Ode   127
The Further-Off-From   96
The Garden of Proserpine   138
The Hyphen   88
The Lady of Shalott: Ode   136
The Needle's   43
The Room   35
The Sentence   26
The Transcendental Aesthetic   104
The White Magician   38
Three Proper   90
Through the Looking Glass   29
Tooth   58
To R.Z. and M.W.   105
Two Other   93
2 Staircase Poems   55

Variations from Sappho   68

Zettel   77

Lightning Source UK Ltd.
Milton Keynes UK
UKHW011842050121
376480UK00001B/261